MW00633541

I believe that what is taught and model[...]
daughters will experience principles of l[...]
profoundly lay the foundation of courage, [...] [...] [...] in their lives.

—BILL THRALL
Co-founder of Trueface and co-author, *The Cure*

If you are a mom who is looking for one practical resource to guide your daughter through her developmental maze from pre-adolescence to healthy womanhood, this is it. *InCourage* is truly one of the best books I have ever read that combines biblical truth with authentic, relatable action steps for moms with young girls. Terra Mattson weaves her beautiful warmth and wisdom into every page as she vulnerably shares her own journey while inviting moms to follow her lead in raising empowered, godly, wise, courageous world-changers!

—Dr. MICHELLE WATSON,
The Dad Whisperer radio host and author of *Dad, Here's What I Really Need from You: A Guide for Connecting with Your Daughter's Heart*

I have known Terra Mattson for more than twenty years. The wisdom and insight of this book comes from personal experience, the hard work of learning, hours of coming along side others as they seek to grow, and careful attention to the wise insights that come from research and education. She has provided a highly accessible and helpful roadmap for helping women of all ages thrive and flourish in a world of increasingly confusing and mixed messages. Let those desiring to raise up a next generation filled with grace and courage pay attention.

—STEVEN G.W. MOORE, Ph.D.
Executive Director, M.J. Murdock Charitable Trust

This book takes an honest look at the complicated worlds of being a daughter and being a mother to these young ladies. Terra brings a unique perspective – as a mother and psychotherapist – to the challenging issue of being a mother and daughter in today's confusing world. InCourage brings an honest look at the importance of courage and grace, and I encourage Christian mothers and daughters to share in its practical wisdom.

—DANIEL SWEENEY, Ph.D., LMFT, LPC
Professor of counseling at George Fox University, practicing therapist, and ordained minister

InCourage

Raising Daughters Rooted in Grace

by Terra A. Mattson

InCourage: Raising Daughters Rooted in Grace
Copyright 2018 by Terra A. Mattson.

All Rights Reserved. No part of *InCourage: Raising Daughters Rooted in Grace* may be reproduced, stored in a retrieval system, or transmitted, in any form or in any means – by electronic, mechanical, photocopying, recording or otherwise – in any form without permission. Thank you for buying an authorized edition of this book and for complying with copyright laws.

THE HOLY BIBLE, NEW INTERNATIONAL VERSION®, NIV® Copyright © 1973, 1978, 1984, 2011 by Biblica, Inc.® Used by permission. All rights reserved worldwide. *Holy Bible, New Living Translation,* copyright © 1996, 2004, 2015 by Tyndale House Foundation. Used by permission of Tyndale House Publishers Inc., Carol Stream, Illinois 60188. All rights reserved. Scripture taken from *The Message.* Copyright © 1993, 1994, 1995, 1996, 2000, 2001, 2002. Used by permission of NavPress Publishing Group.

Living Wholehearted Publishing
www.livingwholehearted.com
www.mycourageousgirls.com

Cover Design by Yvonne Parks || Pear Creative
Author Photo by Julie Fairman || Happenstance Photography

ISBN: 978-1-949709-00-1

Printed in the United States.

DEDICATION

*To my daughters, who are the inspiration for everything I write—
this book started with you in mind. I wanted to write something that
you could hold onto as you develop into women. Keeping the end in
mind, I pray that you will someday hear the heartbeat of my mothering
in the pages of this book and live out its message of grace.*

Table of Contents

Foreword

As a mom of three grown daughters, a grandma to three granddaughters (and a grandson), a pastor's wife ministering over the years to junior high and high school girls, as well as women, and founder of Divine Threads, a ministry reaching out to disenfranchised women, I could not be more excited about Terra's book, *InCourage*.

InCourage could be one of the most important books you will ever read if you are a woman, a mom or a daughter. Terra bravely steps into subjects that need to be addressed, not only personally for each of us, but also together, with our daughters. In a time in history when our identity is threatened on a daily basis, we need a voice louder than our culture telling us the truth of who we are and what we need. *InCourage* does this in very practical ways, giving us both clinical information as well as biblical. Thank you, Terra, for being a woman of courage, willing to step into very difficult subjects with our daughters. May our culture be changed, one girl at a time!

Kathy Towne
Divine Threads Founder
Rolling Hills Community Church
Portland, Oregon

Preface

ABOUT COURAGEOUS GIRLS

This book is a supplement for Courageous Girls groups and is written purposefully for the mamas who lead and participate in them. However, you do not need to start or join a group in order to benefit from the principles and wisdom found in these pages. You may not even have a daughter but find yourself drawn to process your own story as a woman. We were all little girls at one point, right? Among these pages, you will find hope, help, and healing that will transform your own understanding of what it means to live well. Know that this resource stands alone, though you will find many connections and correlations regarding the Courageous Girls material woven into the chapters.

What is Courageous Girls? Knowing the importance of living in community and walking side by side with other moms when I gave birth to my two girls, I found the business of life was always competing with the ideals of my heart. I started Courageous Girls in 2012 for my own daughters and for our local community. God had more in mind, and a movement of Courageous Girls groups started popping up in other parts of the county. Mamas heard about the significance of CG groups and started asking for help. In 2017, I realized that this format and curriculum needed to be available to help mothers navigate the systemic issues plaguing our girls today. With the help of Aimee Eckley, curriculum co-developer, www.mycourageousgirls.com was published as a free resource for any mom and daughter who wants to live with courage and participate in a CG group.

Courageous Girls, LLC is a web-based curriculum equipping moms and daughters to have regular and committed gatherings and to transform lives by fostering confidence, resilience, and grace-filled relationships. Utilizing an ongoing process that incorporates both biblical and clinical inspiration, moms and daughters who participate in Courageous Girls will know the depth and breadth of God's love for them and discover their unique value and purpose along the way. I have found that having regular discussions in safe and personalized environments from early elementary school through high school promotes the development of authentic and strong relationships between girls, mamas, and most importantly, between mothers and daughters. Consequently, these communities help us understand our unique beauty as women and learn how to live a life rooted in grace, identity, purity, purpose, resilience, and courage.

Instead of isolation, Courageous Girls choose community and connection. Instead of worldly input, we seek God's word in our lives. Instead of competition, comparison and judgment, we grow in gratitude, joy and acceptance so that we are equipped to love others well and live our lives from a place of wholeness and grace. It is not a meager task; it is one that requires sacrifice, strength, character and commitment. It is a process that is constantly evolving, especially in our ever-changing, technologically infused lives. As our daughters grow and change, we, too, must adapt the way we connect with them as well as the way we demonstrate love. May you be inspired and encouraged to become a Courageous Girl.

Acknowledgments

Have you ever birthed a baby and recalled all the many supporters who carried you to the finish line? This book was years in the making, and I have been overwhelmed by the gift of encouragement I have received in birthing this "baby."

To my husband, who not only is my best friend and business partner, but who has been the power and faith behind all my dreams—you have helped put feet to my passions. I am so grateful for the ways God loves me well through you. Not only do you keep me laughing and enjoying the little things in life, but you see me in the middle of all my mess. SHMILY.

To my parents, Superpops and Nana (aka, St. Lou) who laid the foundation for who I am today—your commitment to each other and to my sister and me throughout our growing years launched me into living a life of intention. You gave me confidence to be myself, resilience to face hardships, love to hold my feet steady, and fond memories that have become bed time stories for my girls. Mom, you were the first in my life to model what it means to be a Courageous Mama. The influence of your lives will touch more people than you will ever know. Here's to staying cool, calm, and collected. BAEZA! And to my courageous sister, Tiffani, who exhibits many of the principles of this book, thank you for letting me in and for the gift of your laugh! It's the only one that still makes me wet my pants.

To my Courageous Mamas: Ambria, Alicia B., Alicia K., Beth, Heidi, Hollie, Jodee, Janelle, Lisa, and Rachel, who said yes to the crazy idea of a Courageous Girls group—thank you for walking with me as we navigate raising our girls. My unique friendships with each of you have given color to these pages. Your prayers are forever woven into the ripple effect of these words. Thank you for loving me well and allowing me to let my hair down.

To my mother-in-law, Muzzy (and her husband, Papa)—thank you for your prayers, generosity in hosting many years of Courageous Girls retreats, and fostering our CG relationships as moms and daughters. You have been an incredible source of support and encouragement over the years. Here's to Julia Childs impersonations, Muzzy's Marvelous Manners, and for modeling the life of a courageous woman.

To Aimee Eckley, who stepped out in faith when asking me if I would want to get the message of Courageous Girls out to more moms—your willingness to pray, brainstorm, edit, and put countless hours into the CG website and curriculum was used as a catalyst to close the loop for this book. Your fast friendship has been a testimony to how God uses the various gifts of His people for a common purpose.

To my mentors, community, friends, and prayer team, especially Kathy and Christina—your investment has given me a sense of strength, courage, and peace as Jeff and I step out into deeper waters. I am forever grateful for the ways you have freely fanned the flame of our lives and offered wisdom, discernment, and faithful friendship over the many years.

To my clients—thank you for your courage to face the reality of your lives, to step into the process of healing, and to trust me with the most sacred places of your story. You have taught me more than I could ever say in one book and remind me daily of the ways God redeems our pain.

Thank you to our Living Wholehearted team, who partner with us to rebuild, restore, and renew healthy relationships. It is such a joy to shoulder this work together.

To Bill Thralls, Bruce McNicol, and David Pinkerton with Trueface Ministries and the team at NewType Publishings, including my editor, Amanda—thank you for your guidance and belief in this project.

Finally, a humble thank you to God, who not only loves me but by grace has used me to love others. *Your power is made perfect in my weakness.*

Introduction

THE REALITY OF BEING A GIRL

Growing up as an American girl in today's culture takes extraordinary courage. Yet, it seems that the youth of this generation have increasingly less of the traits needed for the challenges before them. The message to "be more," "do more," and "fake it" is pervasive in our nation. From magazine stands to social media messages, from television to textbooks, from our churches to our homes, these messages reflect a condition of our society: we cannot stop striving to gain or greaten our "success." Despite our efforts, our society is not succeeding; we are more depressed, anxious, addicted, self-destructive, and selfish than ever before. We are raised to believe that material success, staying young, remaining healthy, and forming lasting relationships will bring happiness; the truth is, all these things fail us. None of them provides lasting security; though they may cascade in a season, they always run dry over time.

As a mental-health provider and ministry leader with over twenty years of experience, I have witnessed the negative effects of our culture on girls and women of all ages through the stories they share with me. I have been blown away by the storylines they recount, many of which depict the same plot with different characters. In other spaces where people often feel safe to share their experiences, such as educational settings, the stories abound as well. Their lives resemble many of the narratives of my closest friends, my neighbors, and even my own daughters. So often we think the worst-case scenarios only happen to others. Yet, we must know that all of us share in these stories.

I recall one client, a fourteen-year-old, quietly telling me about the numerous boys who had approached her for nude pictures. She shared her stories with a tone of brashness intended to declare her value; to her, the sheer number of boys conveyed her high value among her teenage peers. Like many parents, her mother and father justified her phone use as a "necessary" and convenient communication tool and trusted her to make good choices. They told her that sex before marriage is a sin, but the conversation ended there. Her private Christian school, filled with kids who wanted to please their parents, teachers, and God, was far from equipped to hold this young girl's hand as she walked through the thorn bushes of life. Despite having a good heart and a solid upbringing, she eventually sent pictures of herself unclothed to a boy, who shared it with other male classmates. This increased the pressure to engage in oral sex with several boys whom she "sort of liked." As I listened to her story, my heart broke because she mirrored the same experience of many other girls who explore these challenging situations alone—not because her parents did not care, but because they were simply unaware.

Another young client of mine shared how she could not stop obsessing over photo-shopped Instagram pictures while she counted the calories she put into her body. She cried internally as her dad regularly made jokes about women in public and shamefully commented on female bodies on TV. She secretly battled bulimia and her primary model in life, her mom, battled her own demons around controlling food. She felt trapped in a world that indirectly communicated that worth can only be attained though a certain kind of beauty. Though she loved God, she struggled to know if He loved or even liked her in return. How could God love a girl who was not perfect? He has favorites, right?

Young girls are not the only one's affected by the pressures of modern American culture. A suburban mom shared her story in my office. Like many other women, she told me that she finds herself dreaming of a different marriage each evening after she puts her three kids to bed. She routinely ignores her husband, a workaholic who binges on TV and escapes to pornography late at night, and she finds solace through fantasizing about the lives of others on Facebook and HGTV. Masking depression and panic attacks behind a carefully made-up face, she leads Bible study and mentors young couples in church. A few glasses of wine in the evening take the edge off of her exhausting, lonely life, and she prays that her daughters will have better marriages than she has. She recounted that she feels trapped and alone.

A strong young woman told me her story of being pursued by a high school PE teacher. Though other girls gossiped about her sexual engagements with this instructor, no one offered her help. She never knew how people found out about their relationship, but she felt tremendous shame from their glances and whispers. The teacher, trusted by the community, fed off the girl's distorted view of love: he paid attention to her, which made her feel special. By disguising his sexual abuse as a fulfillment of her own romantic fantasy, he coerced her into a sexual relationship that left scars on her heart and filled her with lies of worthlessness. Even after the relationship ended, she found herself attracted to men who treat her abusively. Ironically, she is an advocate for sex-trafficked girls but cannot see the connection between herself and the survivors she helps in ministry. On the outside, she is a performer whom the world views as a remarkable woman with a bright future. Like the other women whose stories I've shared, she wears the mask well, taking it off only in the sanctuary of my office.

Something has to change.

Today, American girls and women are living divided lives. We are living a reality described by Trueface Ministries as "The Room of Good Intentions."[1] This is a space where we try really hard to be good people and do good things while wearing masks and embracing false identities. In wearing masks, we avoid the depths of our own humanity and miss the very essence of our purpose: to be firmly rooted in grace. Grace transforms us from the inside out, not by our own strength but by God's power and through His love. This is what I want to cultivate in my own family, our community, and across our culture.

The Room of Good Intentions has led to a dismal state of affairs for the girls and women in our nation. Fifty percent of girls in middle school have tried oral sex (many falsely believing that it is the "safe" form of sex). By the time most of these girls are sixteen, they will have had intercourse with at least one person.[2] Sometimes girls in our culture lose their virginity at the hands of multiple partners simultaneously. By the time a woman graduates from college, she is likely to experience one form of sexual assault or abuse, regardless of her background. In a recent study conducted by the Harvard Graduate School of Education, 87 percent of women aged 18-25 years old reported having experienced sexual harassment in their lifetime. Sadly, only 24 percent had ever talked with their parents about how to avoid these situations.[3] Our girls are engaging in far riskier behaviors. Too often, a girl's no holds very little power, as many boys and men have been led to believe she really does not mean it.

Instead of actively teaching girls from a very young age to use their voices boldly, society communicates that they should attract and maintain love and affection from others. Social media, selfie-culture, and instant fame through venues like YouTube, Snapchat, Instagram and reality television, have created a deeply rooted desire for little girls to grow into something "big." Unfortunately, the message to be great is rarely taken to mean aspire to be a rocket scientist, a cure-finder or a great teacher. Instead, the media platforms that engage our youth promulgate the seeming ease and simplicity of becoming an instant Internet sensation, which has superseded the goals of yesteryear. You need only amass a certain number of followers and tweets for the paid promotions and sponsors to foot the bill for life. The danger in girls accepting and believing this cultural truth is the acceptance of the lie behind it: if you are not "somebody," then you are a nobody. This is so far from God's heart.

In a world that offers immediate gratification, one's ability to cope (known as resilience) with anything less than constant satisfaction has plummeted. The rise of self-harming behaviors such as cutting, eating disorders, pornography addictions, and even suicide are at the highest rates across many age groups, and they are rising still. These behaviors are the spoiled fruits from the branches of depression, anxiety, comparison and loneliness. As I counsel women and girls of all ages, the fear of missing out and not being enough is extraordinary. The pain is palpable; they feel stuck between competing demands of how to love ourselves, our families, our friends and significant others while maintaining (with consistent frequency) an image to put forth on social media. This not only affects young girls, but also grown women with life experience, perspective and fully developed brains find themselves trapped in these struggles as well.

Increasingly, younger girls enter the offices of trained professionals across the country to learn how to manage their emotions and conquer the unbeatable game posed by the Room of Good Intentions. It is an epidemic: one in three girls is sexually abused by a "trusted" person in her life; one in two girls thinks her "ideal" body weight is less than she weighs; every single female has been affected by the cultural norms of being "pretty."[4] You may be tempted to believe that this is an exaggeration; doing so certainly makes it easier to live out the status quo. In my years as a therapist, I would actually argue that the numbers are far greater than we know. Over half of the women I work with experienced some sort of covert or overt sexual abuse before the age of eighteen. Most of my clients have only ever shared this truth inside the sacred space of counseling; statistics are based on "reported abuse" that can be quantified and documented publicly.

The reality is that the sex and pornography industries loom over our homes, destroy our marriages, and teach our children that we are merely animals driven by our uncontrolled visceral and primal needs. One only needs to review the ticket sales at the box office for the *Fifty Shades* series to confirm that sex sells. While most women feel nauseous at the thought of being reduced to their body and branded for others to admire and use for their own personal gratification, we still get caught up in the allure of the net cast to catch us and reel us in. We spend billions on beauty products, gym memberships, and, my personal favorite, chin and buttock reconstruction—but for what? So that we will be loved? So that we will be seen? So that someone will notice our beauty and fulfill our longing to be cherished? I believe that what we really (albeit secretly) need to confirm is that we are not alone in our feelings of insecurity and our lack of power. We are all in the same boat and need a way out.

Mamas, get these statistics into your heads! Tear away the veil of indifference or the mantra that you replay in your head that "that's not my daughter." Ask yourself, with brutal honesty, what habits do you engage in that foster feelings of inadequacy in your daughter(s)? It is not easy to identify our shortcomings or weaknesses. However, the cost of avoiding dealing with our own way of being in the world is painstakingly high—and our daughters' resilience and strength depend on it! This book is not meant to scare you into paralysis—quite the opposite. I hope you will be empowered to act and move toward love in order to grow strong and resilient yourself. This is what will help our daughters: being raised by mamas who are actively engaging with and teaching them how to live through life's hardness and filth, holding God's hand every step of the way.

Ladies, you are more than you could ever imagine! You are *not* what society tells you to be. You are *not* what a film producer suggests you should be. You are beautiful and worthy from the moment you are born. You are created with purpose, and that deep longing you feel for love and meaning is freely available and willingly given by your God.

I think loneliness is at the root of most, if not all, unhealthy coping behaviors. When we are confused about who we are and we try to make meaning around the human experience alone, the depths of our souls remain empty. God created us for relationship from the very beginning. His triune character, Father, Son, and Holy Spirit, reflects a Creator who is relational within His very being. As the Genesis account of creation tells in chapter two, we are made in our Creator's image with a desire to be connected. The digital world we live in has made us globally connected, but the ties are held together by a shoe string, and our care for one another has become very fragile over time. This will be addressed further in chapter ten. The point is that our girls are growing up with moms who are lonely and lost too. We desperately need to redefine how we link arms as moms and pursue our daughters in a way that penetrates their God-made souls.

It is time for a movement. Are you in?

You might be thinking, *Yes, but how?*

I get it. Most Christian help is offered with platitudes and ideals (*just pray and trust...*), but it often doesn't explain the crucial next steps. Similarly, most clinical research and self-help books are offered with just that: self-help. A self-help approach is far too limiting. Without something greater than ourselves, we miss the richness of scripture and all God has to offer us. This book aims to fill in the gaps that Christian advice and self-help approaches create by unraveling *how* girls develop a confident voice, a strong sense of self, and a lasting spiritual depth that keeps them rooted throughout the storms of life. Integrating empirically proven clinical wisdom, human development, trauma research, and play therapy with healthy spiritual formation, this book explores the theories, principles and tools you can apply to your ordinary rhythms of life. Soaked in a foundation of biblical truth, my heart is to give you not only a vision for who you and your daughter are meant to be, but also to help draw a road map that weaves transformational principles into the fabric of your relationship.

No one is left out of the pages of this book. Walking with others for many years, I have sat with all kinds of people: prostitutes, pastors, single moms, attorneys, models, surgeons, homemakers, CEOs, millennials, African Americans, Asian Americans, Latina Americans, Middle-Eastern Americans (my own heritage), college students, graduate students, farmers, grass-roots advocates, non-profit founders—you get the idea. Despite our differences, there are fundamental experiences we all share. Regardless of our upbringing, every girl and woman longs to be loved, seen and cherished. Being raised in a Christian home does not guarantee this will happen. According to Bill Thralls, co-founder of Trueface Ministries, the truth is that unless our theology transforms our reality, our children will have a skewed understanding of Father God.[5]

As I held my first daughter at the ripe age of twenty-eight, I had been to four years of college, had finished graduate school (focused on healthy child and spiritual development), and had worked in ministry and clinical environments helping other families with health and healing. Yet nothing prepared me for the gut-wrenching vulnerability that came with knowing all the pain and suffering that my child could endure in this world. I felt so powerless to help her. With prayer, scripture and all my training in relational health and trauma recovery, I wanted to drive this road differently. I even prayed that my children would have just enough "dysfunction" so that they understood the sorrows in this world, but not enough that it paralyzed them from living abundantly and impacting their world. I begged God to hold me tightly as I held my baby tenderly in a world of people who would seek to use her and discard her heart.

As a woman who found my own voice (and started using it) just before I birthed my daughter, I wanted her to recognize her voice early on—to understand her own thoughts, feelings, needs and desires. I wanted her to be able to advocate for herself and others who did not have a voice. I was determined to help my daughter become a girl who knew her value. When my second daughter was born less than two years later, I knew I had been given an enormous task. I prayed this same prayer again, showering her with the same prayers. It was out of this cry that Courageous Girls was born.

When my oldest was in first grade, I made an intentional effort to invite a few other moms into this grand adventure. To my surprise, they said yes! To this day, we are still venturing together, trying to navigate the world of raising girls who know they are loved and who love others well.

Movements start with one voice declaring, "It's time." William Wilberforce, one of the voices in England's slave trade prohibition movement said, "There is no shortcut to holiness; it must be the business of our whole lives." Raising daughters who have a sustained relationship with a personal, loving, and grace-filled God, and who know their purpose in life, requires more than just hope or routine attendance at Sunday morning church services. It requires more than just solid self-esteem and a good education. It requires even more than parents who love their children. Those things are important, but what is really required is laying down our lives for our daughters—

entering into their world to support them and committing ourselves to becoming Courageous Girls alongside them.

The God of the Bible models sacrificial empathy; He left heaven and entered our world through the person of Jesus. This is the same God who rose from the dead and who resides in the form of the Holy Spirit inside every mom who follows Christ. So wherever you are starting, whatever your story, bring all of yourself to the table. You are the key to your daughter's courage. The good news is that the journey of raising our girls is not one we have to walk alone. Instead, we can be empowered by God to accomplish this work as we root ourselves in His grace. Paul's prayer to the church in Ephesians 3:16-21 comes from the same heartbeat that provides life to me and mamas everywhere:

> I pray that out of his glorious riches he may strengthen you with power through his Spirit in your inner being, so that Christ may dwell in your hearts through faith. And I pray that you, being rooted and established in love, may have power, together with all the Lord's holy people, to grasp how wide and long and high and deep is the love of Christ, and to know this love that surpasses knowledge—that you may be filled to the measure of all the fullness of God. Now to him who is able to do immeasurably more than all we ask or imagine, according to his power that is at work within us, to him be glory in the church and in Christ Jesus throughout all generations, for ever and ever! Amen.

This verse has impacted me throughout my adult life. As a young adult of twenty years old, I was conscious to make the most of every opportunity. Determined to avoid passivity, I fervently penned this prayer in my journal:

> *Lord, may You increase and I decrease (John 3:30), may Your power be made perfect in my weakness (1 Corinthians 12:9-10), and may I not only live out the ministry of reconciliation (2 Corinthians 5:18-19), but also know the riches of Your love that You may do far more than I could ever ask or imagine in and through me for generations to come (Ephesians 3:20).*

This prayer, made up of verses that shaped my calling as a marriage and family therapist and my heartbeat for the greater Church, continues to remind me how big God is. My faith is not dependent on me but rather on humbly watching God manifest Himself in the lives of ordinary people. Writing this book and developing Courageous Girls for my own daughters were never aspirations of mine, but they originated from the deep bellows of my soul, compelling me to trust and obey.

I hope that the pages of this book will breathe life, hope, and vision in you as a mother. If you have a Courageous Girls group or want to start one, this book provides deeper dialogue and ways for you to not only grow in your walk with God, yourself, and your daughter, but in your relationship with other moms. At the end of each chapter, you will find suggestions for ways to integrate the principles of this book into your daily life. May this book not only strengthen you but also equip you to understand fully what it means to be *in courage*.

Takeaway

Which struggle do you identify with the most as you read through the stark realities women and girls face today? Consider these questions: *Am I truly willing to look deeper into my own way of being so that I can lead my daughter well? What currently stands in the way of transformation in my own life? Who might I invite along in this journey?* Ask God to guide you as you read through the chapters, showing you the specific principles that apply to your life.

Take It a Step Further

As you consider who your daughter is and who you see her becoming, consider writing a prayer for her from your heart. Give the prayer to her and let her tell you what she might add to your prayer. Pray this prayer together. Consider committing to reading and finishing this book. Consider discussing this book with other moms as part of your own courageous journey.

1

She Walks with Confidence

She is clothed with strength and dignity; she can laugh at the days to come. And she laughs without fear of the future.

- PROVERBS 31:25

If you want to bring a fundamental change in people's belief and behavior...you need to create a community around them, where those new beliefs can be practiced and expressed and nurtured.

— **MALCOLM GLADWELL,** *THE TIPPING POINT: HOW LITTLE THINGS CAN MAKE A BIG DIFFERENCE*

SHE GUARDS HER HEART

As you read this book, my prayer for you is that you would hear the heart behind it. No matter what you may struggle with as a mother or a daughter, I pray that you will know, without any shadow of doubt, that you are loved. I believe that if you deeply understand *agape* love, everything else in your life will flow from that fullness. We can only love others when we ourselves are loved (see 1 John 4:19). We can only give away what we have received. Without love, daily life, and parenting in particular, feels painfully difficult. Christ came to bring us freedom; it is for the sake of freedom (freedom from self-condemnation, shame, fear, and bondage) that I hope you receive these words.

It takes enormous courage to love and be loved well—not the kind of courage we muster for daring acts, such as skydiving or swimming among sharks in the ocean's depths. Those are brave acts, but not the variety that attracts everyone. The word *courageous* means many things in our culture today. Well-known author and sociologist Brené Brown defines it this way: "Courage is a heart word. The root of the word courage is *cor*—the Latin word for heart. In one of its earliest forms, the word courage meant 'To speak one's mind by telling all one's heart.' Over time, this definition has changed, and today, we typically associate courage with heroic and brave deeds."[1] I do not wish to speak about heroism or bravery. The kind of courage I discuss in this book comes from a deep awareness of who we are and to whom we belong. What if we knew that, because of our identity, we are *in courage;* we do not have to produce it on our own. If we knew we always had a safe place to land, along with an endless source of strength, I believe we would be able to venture into unknown territories and live with greater meaning.

Recently, as I was having lunch with a friend and colleague, an elderly man approached our table. His thoughtful stare was noticeable; his eyes were covered with scars. He held the rich wisdom of Oswald Chambers in his hand, a hint of abiding faith in old age. He spoke slowly, with steady intention, as if starting a sermon.

"In courage. In joy. To be in…" He wrapped a piece of paper around his arm, repeating the word "in" and affirming that courage, comfort, joy, and peace are found in the envelopment of God's love. He went on to say, "Enjoy. Encourage." His words flowed from the depths of his soul. If not for the prompting of the Holy Sprit, I might have passed this moment off as a lonely old man merely needing to be heard. However, something inside prompted me to pay attention. My friend and I thanked him for his wisdom, while I pointed to his worn book.

"Are your thoughts from Oswald?" I asked.

He looked me in the eyes and humbly stated, "No, that was from God."

I smiled, goosebumps rising on my skin. He responded with a quiet grin, and, through his crystal blue eyes, I could see a story of one who had been misjudged and overlooked. As he turned to leave, I said, "Thank you and *in*-joy your day." I wanted him to know I had received his point.

A few minutes later he returned to our table to say, "Thank you for listening to my pearls of wisdom." Typically addicted to efficiency and averse to interruption, my manifest patience was a sign of God's presence. "Of course," I replied with a smile. I was struck *again* by how the simple act of listening to another human being can make for holy moments.

What if we lived like we were already *in* courage, content to *in*-joy this life, apart from our own expectations and the expectations of all those around us? What if we modeled this lifestyle for our daughters, and they began to live the same way?

I believe this is the lifestyle of a Courageous Girl. Courageous Girls rest in God's love and keep in step with His way of abundant living. From a biblical perspective, this means she stays in touch with every piece of her heart. She has learned to care for it, nurture it, and recognize what Proverbs 4:23 says about it: "Above all else, guard your heart, for everything you do flows from it." In Old Testament Hebrew culture, the word we translate as "heart" is *lebab*, but it was associated with the core of one's being: mind, body and soul. Another way of expressing the idea might be to say a person's gut or innermost hidden parts. Many times we think *heart* refers to one's emotions, but this is a Western interpretation. When we read this proverb with the Hebrew context, we recognize that we should treat our whole selves like treasured diamonds because all we do and say flows from whatever lies within us—it is the core of who we are.[2]

My daughters have seen many of the inner-workings of who I am—flaws and all. If you are a mom, I imagine you may identify with part of my reality: the cranky mom battling PMS or confronting the cacophony of chores calling to me from every corner of the house; the short-tempered mom, snipping at my husband or struggling to regain composure after telling my girls the same thing repeatedly; the anxious mom, worried about a school event or work project; the fearful mom, troubled about finances and long-term security for my children. My children know what I look like before makeup and how many times I've worn the same outfit multiple days in a row. They have seen me act unkindly with family members during disagreements and have witnessed me giving my husband the silent treatment when my feelings have been hurt. They have seen me grumble, set boundaries, overwork and then crash. They have seen my pride enliven me like a roaring lion and paralyze me like a stubborn mule. They have heard harsh words fly out of my mouth before I could respond to the Spirit's gentle voice—*be slow to speak and slow to anger.* I have not always modeled what I hope my children will know deep down in their hearts—that my love for them will always burn brightly.

But in my broken humanity, my children have also experienced my sincere apology many times over. Asking forgiveness from our children, genuinely and humbly, is a powerful route to connection and trust. This shows them in a tangible, experiential way how God loves us, how we restore when we have done wrong, and how to reconcile with one another. Following repentance, an actual change in behavior pushes me away from sorrow over mistakes made and propels me toward God. Yes, my children have seen my blemishes, but they have also experienced my desperation as I've fallen on my knees to hear the Lord. I desire for my daughters to see me wrestle with authenticity and vulnerability, both of which are difficult to cultivate and critical to healthy relationships. I secretly smile as they peek in on me, quietly sneaking onto my lap for a cuddle as I'm curling up on the couch with my Bible, searching for God's heart, wisdom and truth on good days and bad. I believe my daughters are experiencing me as a real person: one who is leaning into love, surrounding my whole heart with both God and others, while being rooted in courage.

In our often routine, daily life—between laundry, dinner, basketball practice, gymnastics, dog walking and homework—I hope my girls see me courageously standing up for those who are hurting. I want them to experience me loving deeply and grieving wholeheartedly. In the mess, I pray they see the beauty. My courageous mama prayer is that my girls (and your girls, too) will see me modeling what it means to be a woman. The task is daunting, but I know God has honored me with it and therefore I must not take it lightly. Even more, I long to model for them the tangible ways that love overflows from the inside out; when I am filled with *agape* love, I am more likely to trust God's description of me as His child: "fearfully and wonderfully made" (Psalm 139:14, NIV).

We all have a little girl inside us who feels courageous and whom God created to reflect parts of His character to the world around us. We do not need to be perfect. We are not even meant to be "good girls" who make good choices all the time. Courageous Girls are far more than their decisions, actions, words, mistakes, failures and flaws; we are more than our threshold for temptation, and we are more than our sins. My dear friend Dr. Michelle Watson, author and founder of the Abba Project, coined one of my favorite sayings: "My who is not what I do." Try saying it out loud, go ahead. No one is listening aside from that little girl living inside of you. To take it a step further, my who is not defined by anyone other than God, Creator of my life. There is great power in freeing myself from my own expectations and comparison to others. It may sound easy, but we know it is not. There is something in our female DNA that simply cannot resist checking out the woman in line in front of us and comparing ourself to her. The urge to find fault with another woman is real and often leaves us struggling to create authentic friendships and maintain healthy, fulfilling and edifying relationships.

SHE VISITS ELI

Max Lucado wrote many of our family's favorite storybooks. One of the most frequently read books in our home is *You Are Special*.[3] It's about a town of wooden people who spend their days sticking dots and stars on one another. Those who make mistakes, are less attractive, or perform poorly compared to others receive black dots. Those who are pretty and perform well receive gold stars.

The story's main character, Punchinello, is constantly covered with dots and feels unworthy. One day, he meets a girl who does not have any dots or stars on her body, so he asks her to reveal her secret. Lucia tells him to visit Eli, the maker of all the wooden people. Punchinello visits Eli and finds himself at the feet of a loving carpenter who delights in his presence, despite Punchinello's dots. As Punchinello receives love from Eli, one of his dots falls to the ground. Eventually, Punchinello learns there is no special formula for removing dots. Instead, relationship with the maker reminds each wooden person how uniquely special they are and the security that comes from his love trumps the stickers' power and relevance.

Hopefully, you can see Lucado's metaphor. When we, as flawed individuals, spend time with our Maker, we are able to focus on how He values us and are less likely to possess self-limiting perspectives. While no one enjoys receiving "dots" from their peers, it is certainly tempting to accept "stars" when they're being handed out—Student of the Month, Player of the Year, Employee of the Quarter; life has a way of keeping us tethered to stars with an ever-growing list of ways to earn them. Have you bought into this? Are you striving to earn the praise of another person? Are you working to excel at something so that you can achieve a higher "rank" or more publicity? Think in terms of our children's daily experiences. They have certainly bought into the world of stars and dots, undoubtedly because there is a deep hunger in our culture for stars. Why do they desire this kind of praise? Sadly, the more we hand out stars, the more our children thirst for them. Over time, this thirst grows into an insatiable need that won't go away (no matter how many Instagram followers you get).

The serious problem with this mindset is that we cannot have one without the other. By choosing to accept the stars when people offer them, and proudly wearing the symbol so that others can see how "worthy" we are, we are, by default, posturing ourselves to accept the dots. We may try to refuse them, but they still stick. There is no shortage of dots, is there? We do not even need to list them; your mind (and likely your daughter's mind) is full of them already. Moms, heed this warning: it only takes our children accepting one dot to destroy the hundreds of stars they may have already accumulated.

As mothers, we work hard to fortify our girls with compliments. We teach that "words can't hurt," though everyone of us knows words can be like daggers. We try to armor them with the "right" clothes to wear to school to prevent verbal teasing or being left out. In trying so hard, we are still perpetuating the cycle of human-driven approval. Essentially, we hand out stars to our girls from birth in hopes to keep them from receiving dots. In our society, it's really hard to escape others' attempts to tag us with dots or stars (or, in the world of social media, thumbs up or thumbs down). Though this human approval system is not new, it has become instantaneous.

The "sticker trap" imprisons us in a performance-based cycle of rewards and consequences. Sometimes, this approach is repackaged as the tenets of Christianity, the "shoulds" and "should-nots" of the faith. But I am certain this is *not* what Jesus intended to impart to His people. Jesus never wielded judgment over productivity levels or assessed people by their achievements. He did tell parables about using our gifts and talents, but He did not keep tally marks of who earned stars and who received dots to determine the love and attention He offered. God does not have favorites and His love is not based on our merits.

Let me clarify that words of affirmation and verbal compliments *are* important. Freely offering life-giving words of encouragement is vital and key to healthy development. Every girl still needs to hear that she is beautiful, smart, generous, or kind, though her worth is not based on such attributes. When we gift our daughter with words that speak to her value, regardless of performance, she will be able to release the power of stars and dots.

So, how do we help our kids find their worth from their Maker's point of view alone? It starts with us—parents. We begin by teaching our children that their value is *only* defined by the unconditional loving God who knit them in the womb. You can teach this directly or indirectly to your daughter, but only if you accept the truth yourself. How you believe the Creator views you will translate into what you prioritize in your life. In a world that battles this concept every second, we must remind our daughters (and ourselves) daily to return to the Creator—through prayer, meditation, singing, playing, reading His Word, using our talents to serve, and enjoying life. These are ways in which God intentionally pursues our heart. Remember, it is God's job to brush off the stickers that have been thrust upon us. While we cannot control who tries to put a sticker on us or our girls, we can determine whether or not the dots and stars retain their adhesive power. We do this by recognizing that we are created with purpose by a God who loves us and sees us as worthy through His Son, Jesus. The more we connect with "Eli," the more we can prevent the world's stickers from sticking.

Lucia, the female character in Max Lucado's story, is a terrific example of a Courageous Girl. She beautifully depicts one who chooses relationship with her Creator over definition by the other wooden people in her town. Lucia's relationship with Eli frees her to be all she is made to be. Sure, she stands out, but in doing so she points others to Eli so that they too can be free from the "sticker trap."

The sticker trap burdens us with the three sabotages of true intimate relationship: shame, ego, and pride. In contrast, the "maker mindset" develops our resiliency against the temptation to accept outside judgments and pronouncements of worth. Developing maker-mindset resilience is hard to accomplish in today's world, but it is not impossible. The world is quickly changing, but the hard evidence of the great gospel message has never changed. I am confident that God's desire is not only to recognize our unmet needs but also to draw us close to Him, as daughters, so that we can be deeply loved. Our daughters will learn how to receive the love of God as they practice alongside us. We are their first example of God as a relational, loving being.

SHE LIVES LIFE

As our children's primary caretakers, we are their first relationship models. Our relationships with our children communicate the loudest message of who God is and who they are. Our daughters will spend much of their adulthoods either living out the messages we impart or trying to free themselves from them. Whether I am cuddling with my daughters on the couch or running around the house preparing for the next Courageous Girls gathering, I try to consider every moment an opportunity to disciple them. In all things, I am called to share, communicate and demonstrate the love of God to my family.

Here's the catch: I cannot be everything to everyone else *and* disciple my children well. No one can. Many try and fake it well for a while, but eventually something must be sacrificed on the altar of life. We try to juggle the endless demands and expectations of the world around us instead of stepping into the sweet spot for which we are uniquely designed. Competing priorities pull at us, promising that if we put our energies in certain endeavors, we will find fulfillment. Christians have even made up another set of standards that falsely promise a 1-2-3 step plan: "If you..., then..." The truth is that there is *nothing* we can do to satisfy the world's expectations or guarantee outcomes, and yet we still try. It's a dead-end trap to keep us frustrated and striving for validation. This way of thinking destroys us and distracts us from truly living.

In my life, letting go of this lifestyle has meant surrendering and accepting my specific call in life for today: to partner with my husband in our business; to see clients a couple days a week; and to mother my girls intentionally through the treacherous waters of public school alongside a few other moms and daughters. I have stopped comparing myself to the blogging supermom and the Mother Teresa homemaker, though God bless them both!

For some moms, surrender means stepping down from a position at work. For another, it looks like working hard outside the home to make ends meet and put food on the table. For another, it looks like appreciating her marriage and small home while mothering three children and homeschooling. We do not need to do it all or be it all. We are only called to be our authentic self, and it takes time to discover who that is. Social media will not tell us the answers but only provides ideas, inspiration, and, at times, sensory overload. We each have our own way of being the mom our girls need to see, and the only way we know our personal path is to spend time connecting with our own heart and the heart of God.

Fill in the blank in the following sentence based on something that feels true for your experience: "If I am not _____, then I am not enough." Most of us can fill that space with several words that lead us to believe we are falling short. Here are some common answers: "running my business well," "attending the PTA fundraiser," "spending enough time with each child," "sending out Christmas cards to my family and friends," "providing permanent shelter for my children," "fitting into my jeans," "going to church," "cooking a nutritious dinner every night for my family." The list goes on and on. How we answer this statement helps us determine where we find our identity and worth.

As you consider your statement, it's important to remember that lies, shame statements and distractions are not the truth that God speaks over us. We are made in the image of God, and His uniquely ordained purpose rests upon each of us. There is no other *you* on the planet. There is no one else like your daughter. Carolyn Leaf, a brilliant Christian neurologist and author, says it this way: "You make a lousy me, and I make a lousy you."[4] No matter what motherhood has stripped away or added to your job description, no matter how many days end in tears kissing your baby's forehead because you arrived home after her bedtime, no matter what your neighbor posts on Facebook about the camps she sends her kids to in the summertime, you cannot live your life comparing yourself to others. The only way to settle this deeply human desire to compare ourselves is to turn our focus to God, follow what He calls us to do, and grow in the ability to celebrate what He is doing in others. It is so hard—but so good.

Get quiet. Can you hear God whispering? What purpose has He given you for this moment—not for tomorrow, but for today? Here's the simplest way I can summarize God's response to me when I ask Him this question: to be courageous by being myself. It is a courageous act to be loved as I am and to love others as they are. I cannot do this perfectly, but when I can overflow out of my relationship with my Creator, I am enabled for courage. More importantly, I am equipped to enter into the hearts of my daughters so that I can walk with them at every stage of life.

SHE LIVES IN TODAY

How do we know how to enter into relationship with our girls, especially if they are transitioning through a difficult stage of development or struggling with issues we never experienced in childhood (hello, iPhones)? The world offers many suggestions and well-meaning manuals to address this question. Some parenting models allow children to experience life on their own, entirely independent from their parents. "They won't learn unless they experience it themselves." An alternative extreme protects children from everything, so they enter the world without any life experiences outside those ordained by parents. Both philosophies leave our daughters vulnerable.

Following the wisdom of two of the world's leading experts in play therapy, Dr. Daniel Sweeney and Dr. Garry Landreth, I adhere to this approach: "Do not do for a child what they can do for themselves."[5] This principle helps children develop deep inner confidence unrelated to the praise of others. This principle also teaches adults the importance of recognizing and educating ourselves about our children's current developmental stage. When we make ourselves attentive to our children, we can help them build skills and confidence, allowing them to practice new things or test new ideas within the safety of a relationship filled with love and limits. Being courageous mamas who invest in their Courageous Girls means we must take time to know our daughter's unique way in the world, help her build skills, and give her ways to practice and develop confidence within the safety and security of grace. This requires allowing extra time for mistakes, practice, and innovation.

To be truly honest, I struggle daily to prioritize this principle as well. The temptation to do things for our children or miss an opportunity to come alongside them to encourage and train is far too easy in light of our busy lives. I still feel mommy guilt at times for doing something for myself or for serving various ministries instead of my family. I know the pressure to cook a nutritious meal so that my kids' memories of dinnertime are not only mac-n-cheese and reheated chicken nuggets.

The reality of pausing long enough to look into my daughters' eyes at least once a day requires intentionality. I am slowly learning that the balance of living out who I am *and* being a Courageous Mama are one and the same. I am still in the process of learning how to accept that where I am is where I am supposed to be—a message I want all Courageous Girls to embrace. Grace meets us where we are and helps us grow from there.

There is so much to learn about being a daughter of the King of grace. The Bible tells us that each woman has purpose and is uniquely made and equipped to fulfill it. Fulfillment of this truth is developed by spending time with God, sinking her roots into the truth that she is loved and boldly offering that love to others. This is what it means to be a Courageous Girl. Courageous Girls come in all shapes and sizes, but the core of who she is becoming can be summed up in the following acronym:

C - Confident in who God made her to be

O - Open to those who are different than her

U - Understands and applies God's Word in daily life

R - Risks because her faith is in a big God

A - Asks for help (both in the form of personal prayer and within her community)

G - Generous with her time and resources

E - Empathetic

O - Obedient to God

U - Unique from the world around her

S - Servant-hearted

G - Good friend (even when it's hard)

I - Initiates with integrity

R - Real and honest with God and others

L - Lives and loves wholeheartedly

Finally, Courageous Girls are present. They are committed to continually shedding others' expectations and fight to be in the here and now. They are responsible, fully in tune with the Spirit, and bear fruit because of their relationship with Him.

> But the fruit of the Spirit is love, joy, peace, patience, kindness, goodness, faithfulness, gentleness, self-control; against such things there is no law. And those who belong to Christ Jesus have crucified the flesh with its passions and desires. If we live by the Spirit, let us also keep in step with the Spirit. Let us not become conceited, provoking one another, envying one another. (Galatians 5:22-25, NIV)

Paul spent many of his Epistles urging both Jews and Greeks to live with freedom so that they would not be overcome by the sin, strife and immaturity rampant in their culture. The church of Ephesus had been swept away by strong socio-cultural influences, and the church of Galatians was caught up in legalistic rules and doctrines adhered to prior to Christ. Sound familiar? Being a Courageous Girl is not for the faint of heart, but for those who desire to be like Lucia—uninhibited by dots *or* stars—totally free. It is difficult to live like we are truly loved. It is even harder to teach others to do this. It is a muscle that must be strengthened through practice and transferred to our children in ordinary moments from the abundance of love we have received.

The following chapters unveil practical steps and activities for both you and your daughter to live like you are loved so that you both can embrace courage. If practiced, they will help you create space for slow and steady shifts in your relationship. Spend a little time each day cultivating these important action steps and consider discussing noticeable changes with other moms as you choose to live courageously.

Takeaway

Make a list of five attributes you notice and adore in your daughter and five attributes you notice and appreciate about yourself. Try to keep your list focused on your God-given attributes (like wisdom or attention to detail) instead of temporary traits (like good grades or athletic achievements). Once you have a list, pray over these traits daily. Keep them by your bedside and ask God to develop them in your daughter. Ask Him to use these qualities to protect her and build her resilience. Pray that you would both see these gifts in connection with her God-given purpose and that she would be drawn to God's design for her with clarity and enthusiasm. Remember, she is on a long journey to discover who God made her to be.

Take It a Step Further

Ask your daughter to write down five traits that she believes God gave her on purpose. How does her list compare to your list? Talk about what each of you wrote and how she shows her gifts in your family, to her friends and to the outside world. If you can, model this activity for your daughter. Allow yourself to be vulnerable to your daughter and share something you believe God gave you that is helping you live out of your greater purpose.

2

She Embraces Holy Crap

The Spirit of the Sovereign Lord is on me, because the Lord has anointed me to proclaim good news to the poor. He has sent me to bind up the brokenhearted, to proclaim freedom for the captives and release from darkness for the prisoners, to proclaim the year of the Lord's favor and the day of vengeance of our God, to comfort all who mourn, and provide for those who grieve in Zion—to bestow on them a crown of beauty instead of ashes, the oil of joy instead of mourning, and a garment of praise instead of a spirit of despair. They will be called oaks of righteousness, a planting of the Lord for the display of his splendor. They will rebuild the ancient ruins and restore the places long devastated; they will renew the ruined cities that have been devastated for generations.

- ISAIAH 61:1-4 (NIV)

I live several miles outside of town in the quiet hills of Oregon wine country. Not so long ago, the region where I live was home to a rural farming community. Given the environment, I enjoy raising small animals with my family—dogs, cats, chickens, and so forth—so I know the smell of manure. Often while doing my chores, God has given me fresh analogies to apply to life's less-than-fragrant moments.

Several years ago, I received an impression that life sometimes feels like a huge pile of dung. There might be better words to explain this feeling, but the sense is widely understood: none of us can escape life's difficult moments. In many cases, the term "crap" feels like an enormous understatement when describing life on Earth. The realities and consequences of abuse, addiction, shame, bondage and brokenness can feel so heavy at times that we double over in prayer, begging they will stop.

Scripture tells us that the heart is deceitful (see Jeremiah 17:9) and that all of us fall short of God's glory (see Romans 3:23). All of us! The fall has affected so many aspects of our human existence. So why are we surprised when hard things happen in our lives? Why do we believe that our crap falls singularly on our shoulders and that our lives are the only ones that stink at times?

Some Christians teach the idea that if we experience anxiety, sadness, exhaustion, depression, anger, envy or bitterness because of life's difficulties, we do not trust God enough. I recently sat in the audience of a well-respected conference and heard one of the speakers share from the microphone that it is a "sin to feel despair." I could not disagree more. Try telling that to a mother who has lost a child to cancer or lost a marriage because of her husband's addiction to pornography. This kind of theology causes us to hide, covered by and cowered in shame, and increases our despair.

The mentality sounds a little like that of Job's friends, who asked him what he did to deserve the pain he was experiencing. According to Job 1:8, Job was "blameless—a man of complete integrity. He feared God and stayed away from evil." Job's three friends, Eliphaz, Bildad, and Zophar, tried to comfort Job with their presence after he lost everything— his family, his livelihood, and his health. In their attempt to care for Job, they told their friend that the suffering he was experiencing was his fault, and they instructed him to repent. Job responded, "You are miserable comforters, all of you!" (Job 16:2). Too often we falsely think that the plight of our pain (or someone else's pain) or the blessings in our life are directly correlated to God's judgment of our behaviors. "What goes around comes around" is not a premise of Christianity.

I have heard this theology again and again in my office as women blame themselves for suffering in their lives. Some of it does belong to the natural consequences of one's choices, but not always. This theology seeps into our homes when we ask our daughter what she did to provoke the bully on the playground or blame her for the violation she experienced while under the influence at a party. We fear telling another person about our struggles because, rather than receiving empathy, we're afraid we will be told we lack faith. The truth is, we all have struggles. There is a subtle balance between recognizing the smell of crap before we can acknowledge the miracle of transformation into something holy. Life throws us unexpected curveballs, but God is still good and meaning can still come out of the messes.

SHE BELIEVES GOD USES ANYTHING

Years ago, when diaper changes and toilet training were part of our family's daily routine, my husband and I longed for the day when "poop" was not a regularly used word in our home. The word became so entrenched in our vocabulary that God used it to give me clarity about relational and spirituals matters. In that season, I pondered the purpose of poop and its role in our development as healthy people and mature disciples. My farmer friend, Beth, also known as the "egg lady" in my neck of the woods, contemplated with me the ways in which farming teaches biblical principles. As you could probably guess, poop plays a significant role in the agricultural system. Manure is highly valued by farmers who want to produce a robust harvest. It is incredibly nourishing. It turns out that the by-product produced from all living animals (poop) turns into a rich supply of vitamins and minerals that, when tilled into the soil, make for stronger, thriving plants. Who knew that poop could be so essential to growth? What we consider "waste" in our lives, and often want to get rid of, God uses to nourish us in deeper ways. The crap we experience in life can either sit useless and stink or it can become some of the best nourishment for our soul.

Solomon, one of the wisest men in the Bible, boasted great riches and enjoyed all the pleasures of life. However, in Ecclesiastes he presents an ironic and unexpected truth:

It is better to go to a house of mourning than to go to a house of feasting, for death is the destiny of everyone; the living should take this to heart. Frustration is better than laughter, because a sad face is good for the heart. The heart of the wise is in the house of mourning, but the heart of fools is in the house of pleasure. It is better to heed the rebuke of a wise person than to listen to the song of fools. Like the crackling of thorns under the pot, so is the laughter of fools. This too is meaningless. Extortion turns the wise into fools and bribe corrupts the heart. The end of a matter is better than its beginning, and patience is better than pride. (Ecclesiastes 7:2-8, NIV)

In this passage, Solomon suggests that searching for wisdom and understanding in life's hardships far exceeds seeking pleasure and comfort. Death as destiny sounds gloomy, but I have seen how those who embrace mourning and acknowledge their own fragility tend to enjoy the pleasures they are given far more than those who choose to ignore the "poop" or try to live above life's trials. Often, these wise travelers are able to move through pain by embracing the grief that comes along with it, and emerge on the other side richer and more resilient. Abundant living is learning to embrace *all* of life.

I recall regular conversations with one of my dear friends, Christina. For years, she and her husband longed for children but struggled with infertility. I remember our conversations about people who made insensitive comments out of naïveté—easy pregnancies and multiple babies can lead one to believe that it is a simple process. People often take having a baby for granted until a ten-year journey turns the desperate effort into a job rather than a romantic endeavor. After several years of fertility treatments, in-vitro fertilization miraculously brought them a child, a precious girl. For their second child, they moved forward with plans to adopt, knowing how unlikely another conception would be. However, the adoption took years longer than they imagined because of international government bureaucracy. They experienced more waiting. More disappointment. More *poop*.

They agreed to consider adopting a baby with special needs. They simply wanted to hold the child God had intended them to love. As has been the case with several women I know, Christina became pregnant after bringing home their adopted daughter. This time, the pregnancy occurred without any human interventions. I believe that years of infertility challenges resulted in this family placing a high and rightful value on their children, far more than most. Each daughter is a miracle in her own right, and my friend has responded to these gifts with great, intentional parenting, such that only comes from knowing the depth of pain and sorrow that preceed blessing. She is a beautiful example of a mom who turned life's manure into something holy.

Walking alongside clients and friends through seasons of drought has showed me that no one wants to be alone in brokenness. Part of the spirit of Courageous Girls is to create community through slow, steady, trusted relationships by establishing safe spaces where authenticity and vulnerability (showing our "poop") can be practiced without the risk of rejection. Three things allow this to take place: honesty, mercy and love. This is how God works, both in and through us. Dr. Harville Hendrix says, "We are wounded in relationships. But we are healed in relationships."[1] Honesty allows God, and others, to see our crap; it also brings awareness to how good, gracious, loving and creative our God is. He takes poop and uses it to grow us.

As we hear the intimate details of another person's life story, there is temptation to oversimplify our response or move through it quickly, especially if it involves pain or discomfort. Many well-intentioned mentors, friends, loved ones and pastors can get trapped sharing biblical rhetoric that falls flat on the recipient. They might say true statements like "God has a plan," or "He will use this," but the timing of sharing those words just wasn't right. Yes, the Bible offers promises we can and must cling to in turbulent waters. Jesus is most definitely our truest friend, in calm times and in the midst of any storm. However, sharing these truths in the midst of a person's raw pain must be tempered. Otherwise, it's too hard to hear and can feel minimizing, devaluing and dismissive of one's personal story. This kind of trite response can send someone further away from God rather than drawing her closer to Him.

From women who have been betrayed in their marriages to mothers who have lost children to suicide or tragic accidents, rhetoric is not enough. Their situations cannot be explained away with a verse or a well-meant poem. These stories are war stories; many of us carry them, some more quietly than others. There is really no other way to hear these stories than to sit side by side with a survivor and bear witness to her journey. As a client of mine once said, we try to put marble over dry-rot with words, but they fall short. Like rich fertilizer, time and presence allow the nutrients from manure to seep deep into the ground before the fresh green blades of grass make an appearance. We must, at least for a winter season, let ourselves face the hard parts of our stories in order to look back and see how God's always-protective hand carried us through the eye of the storm.

SHE MOVES THROUGH SATURDAY: A TIME OF MOURNING

Revisiting and grieving our pain *with Jesus* and the gentle help of others is the only path to resurrection, victory and redemption. The road map has been laid out well for us. As believers in Jesus Christ, our faith is founded on the idea that resurrection comes through suffering, death, and grief. There is no way to Sunday but through Saturday. John Ortberg explores this idea further in his devotional on despair and joy.[2] Not only did Jesus face death in all its reality, but He remained in the tomb for three days before He rose to overcome the death sentence. His followers' devastation must have been gut wrenching: not only did their promised Messiah suffer a criminal's death, but they were being hunted by Jesus-haters. One moment they were sitting at the feet of their Messiah, and the next moment they were living in fear and despair without any awareness that Resurrection Sunday was coming. They lived through Saturday—the day between Jesus' death and His resurrection. It was a day of unknown proportions, between the messiest of all messes (Good Friday) and pure holiness (Easter Sunday). Heavy with uncertainty, Saturday was a day of mourning.

As humans, we must mourn. We must grieve. We must learn to accept what we think is a waste and allow it to mix into the good so that it can become a part of our soul's nourishment. The tapestry behind our journey is often a wad of knots that we do not want others to see. There is no point trying to keep the two extremes of our lives separate: one holy and pure, the other failures and darkness. This is where clinical practice and scientific wisdom meet the biblical truth of grace and redemption. Grieving is a skill most of us do not possess, until we are forced to practice it. Even then, we often want to minimize our feelings, push them away, or mask them. A gentle reminder, sweet mama: hard hearts equal soft faith. Only through softening our heart and feeling all of the agony of grief does our faith have a chance to flourish. The true equation is this: soft hearts equal stronger faith!

Over the years, one of the most common questions I hear from clients is "How long will this take? One, two, or three sessions?" Like Dorothy and her glittery red slippers, we want to click our heels together and send all the pain away in a big tornado of darkness. The problem with poop is that no matter how far away it flies, or how well it is hidden, you can always smell it! I once heard a story from a kids' ministry leader in a nearby church who served with the 3-year-olds on Sunday morning. One Sunday morning, the kids were playing in the church classroom when the teacher smelled a foul odor in the air. She followed her nose to a corner of the room where a little boy was happily building a tower out of brightly colored blocks. The odor grew stronger. She bent down and asked the little boy if he needed to use the bathroom. "No," he replied calmly, without looking up from his masterpiece. Just then, the teacher noticed a little pile of poop next to the boy. He had not wanted to stop his project to use the bathroom, so he left it in the corner assuming someone else would clean up his business! Let this be a lesson to us all: if you let your poop sit unattended, it will not only turn into a bigger mess, but it will make a mess of other people's lives too. This is a humorous story, but the implications are less amusing. The hurts of life can turn us into people who hurt others or refuse to be loved in return, whether we mean to or not. When you willingly step toward processing your pain and grieve in healthy ways, something beautiful emerges—*you,* as God intended you to be. Courage to let go of the past allows us to open our hands and embrace what is and what could be. This takes time.

I am often asked, "What's the point of revisiting or ruminating on the pain of the past? Won't that make my experience worse?" This question comes frequently from the teachers, police officers, pastors, counselors, nurses and physicians that sit in my office. Interestingly, they are some of the bravest in our community. They live their lives to help others, but when it comes to their own story, they give themselves very little permission to heal. The reason many of these people are so successful within their careers is because they are exceptional at dissociating, a term used in the clinical world to explain when a person separates themselves from a stressful or traumatic event in order to survive it. Like traveling a regular route home and not remembering you stopped at a stop sign or red light, dissociation is a way to coast through life without being emotionally present. God created dissociation as a means to help us cope in the most horrific of moments, but the brain will not shut down this coping strategy until we have confirmed the safety of ourselves or others. When someone has experienced trauma, he or she learns to sail through life above the waves so that they are not caught in the undertow of emotions lying in the depth of their souls. But remember, the waves and wind are often the very things that can bring us closer to God. Isaiah 61 reminds us that this is why Jesus came: to heal the brokenhearted and to bring comfort to those who mourn.

Think about it: if we are totally honest, we're all pretty good at dissociating. New mothers tend to their infants day and night, even after lengthy and challenging births, despite functioning on extremely low levels of rest. This trauma affects a mother's body, yet each day she does it again. Community helpers and leaders take care of others because they have a high tolerance for trauma. The problem is that dissociating never allows for resolution, which means that a person's body, brain and soul are continually processing pain that eventually and inadvertently leaks into other parts of life. What parts of your history have been sealed shut or are not permitted to surface? What stories or lies do you carry deep inside that catch you off guard? These are the experiences that need to be faced; we must grieve the losses so that we will be able to have compassion for another. Dismissing our own pain leads to dismissing the pain of our loved ones around us. The illusion of skipping Saturday and jumping miraculously from Friday to Sunday is not only unhealthy but may actually signal unresolved trauma. Modeling to our daughters that a Courageous Girl accepts mourning as a necessary part of emotional health reveals the ways God renews devastated places.

SHE WAITS FOR SUNDAY: A TIME OF REJOICING

Saturday was a day of grieving, but then Sunday came—and with it, the resurrection and restoration promised. Imagine being one of the disciples at the time of Jesus' death. After such despair on Saturday, the empty tomb turned their mourning into rejoicing. Death could not hold Him down. In the darkness of our mess, when resurrection Sunday feels too far away, we still hold onto the promises of paradise where we are promised there is no more sin, no more tears, and no more death. In moments of confusion and guttural sorrow, I long for heaven.

While raising daughters in a world full of crap, we can cling to the hope of heaven. We must hold onto God's greater story and teach it to our girls. I've poured over the pages of my well-worn Bible looking for God's exact play-by-play. How do I protect my daughters' hearts from the inevitable pain of this life? How do I get us around Saturday and make it to Sunday? Friends, we cannot get to Sunday on our own. Our grief, loss, regret and pain will hold us in Saturday until we give it back to the One who can redeem and repurpose it. Jesus is who He says He is—the one who came for the sick and sinner, not the well. He is the only professed Messiah in history who actually rose from the dead and conquered death. He is the only One whose nails pinned sin to the cross, but not the spirit. He is the only One who can take all the crap in our lives and, somehow, make it holy. This far exceeds our abilities. Though we may try to heal our hurt or the hurt of others, that is not our job. We can never accomplish this on our own. We will never think or feel or cry our way to healing. Our hope must rest in Him alone.

God is in the business of transforming death and hopelessness into resurrected life and new beginnings. Isaiah 61 says we will receive a double share in the place of shame. Our daughters desperately need to understand this in the core of their beings. They need to watch us experience this kind of powerful transformation as we work through our own grief and pain with Jesus. So often, we only let our daughter see the resolved version of ourselves, but she never gets to witness our growth process. This is critical to her ability to recognize and normalize her own humanity. She will see the difference in us when our heart has been healed; she will feel the peace that exists when our soul is finally at rest.

Let's surround ourselves with those who are honest and real—those who surrender the masks of measuring up in exchange for the authenticity of grace and forgiveness. Let's become these women and walk alongside others in this journey. In the words of Francesca Battistelli in one of my favorite songs, "Bring your brokenness, and I'll bring mine. 'Cause love can heal what hurt divides. And mercy's waiting on the other side…if we're honest."[3]

SHE IS HONEST

One of the greatest gifts of having a Courageous Girls group is an intentional safe space where moms help one another consistently work through the crap in their lives. This space is grace, because it's the extension of undeserved favor given again and again. Part of this process involves casting out fears of the unknown, fears that we naturally feel as mothers and as women. These fears can be driven by sensationalized media and world views that suggest we have no authority over our children and no basis to hope for a better future. The fears can come from our own life experiences that have taught us that we are powerless and unheard. This lie was already defeated by Jesus. The truth is that we can absolutely influence our daughters' lives by being connected and maintaining strong, meaningful relationships with them. By freeing ourselves from paralyzing fear, we can keep our trauma from leaking into our daughters' lives while we help them navigate paradigms differently. We can do this because of Jesus' love and power in and through us. Let's invite God to work in us and cast out the fear with which we wrestle. Let's live out new paradigms with our children and teach them to do the same. When our daughters practice honesty with us, may we handle their vulnerability with great care and show them that honesty breeds wholeness.

SHE HAS GRACE

Have you ever felt like the house never truly gets clean? Or, once you clean it up, it becomes messy again? Have you gardened before and recognized that the weeds always return? *What's the deal?* One of the lies we have accepted is that the more mature we become in Christ, the less crap one has. I don't know about you, but it doesn't make logical sense to me. I think that if we asked Farmer Beth about her livestock, she would say that as long as her animals are living, they are producing manure. As all mamas know, our children never stop pooping. I think maturing in Christ and becoming healthy, courageous women is more about knowing what to do with our poop than it is about not having any.

My husband built me the most beautiful chicken lodge I could imagine. And while it's wonderful to have farm-fresh eggs in the morning, there is always more chicken poop than there are eggs. Being human means that my sin, my pain, my brokenness and my struggles are all God's to use for His purposes. I see it daily. But just like chicken waste becomes highly valuable fertilizer once it has been metabolized and processed, our brokenness can be transformed to nourish the soul. Maybe the message we should promulgate, and that aligns more with gospel-centered truth, is that Jesus is in the business of resurrecting, returning and repurposing what the enemy has tried to kill, steal and destroy.

One of the Courageous Girls groups I lead has been extremely challenging and messy. These groups are not free of issues, but that's the point. Right now, we are battling hard things like mean-girl behaviors and healthy communication habits (even within the group) that will help these women guide and coach their daughters toward healthier relationships. We are all in process, and it is our job to coach our girls. The pain of being human continues to sting. And yet I am convinced that this kind of environment is critical; we need to practice being less judgmental and less decisive about who we are or are not and who others are or are not. The reality is that we are all made up of the potential for good and bad. Genesis 1:27 teaches that males and females were made in God's image and that we are a beautiful reflection of the glorious ways of God. However, when given free will, it seems we often choose a path of destruction. We become discontent, curious, strong-willed and prideful. Dealing with the consequences of the choices we make and the behaviors we embrace, particularly in family and community, is difficult.

Teaching our daughters how to be honest about their thoughts, emotions, behaviors and needs happens in a safe environment with a sturdy foundation where pain can be used for character-building and maturing. Safety is felt when we feel that we can show all of ourselves without being judged, defined, or forced to pretend. It is solidified when we sit and process together. The first step in building a safe relationship with our daughters is to be honest as moms and to allow our daughters to be honest with us. A foundation of trust is built, and they will come to us again. When they feel they can tell us anything without being met with immediate judgment, criticism, withholding of love, or hijacking of our emotions, they will grow up to know what grace looks and feels like with God and others.

This does not mean that our job is to be totally permissive parents who never discipline our children or give consequences. What this means is that, *first*, we listen to their hearts. We don't react immediately. We are slow to speak, quick to listen. We do not rush to judgments or assumptions. We do not worry about how our children's actions will reflect on us or how others perceive us. We listen and create space where they can be heard, and we get them the help they need. We regulate our emotions. This practice is intentional and requires great awareness on our part, but it reflects God's character in the flesh. And when we blow it, we own it and make it right. Play-therapy expert Dr. Landreth says it this way: "It's not always what you do, but what you do after what you did that matters most."[4] Our faith is founded on repentance and forgiveness. Life from death. Beauty out of ashes. Grace is the only way.

SHE RECEIVES GRACE

When my youngest was five, she confessed that she had been hiding my husband's most treasured cookies, the Christmas Spritz. Jeff's mom gives him bags full of Spritz cookies every Christmas, and Jeff hides them in the freezer to last throughout the winter nights. Covered in Spritz cookie crumbs and greasy finger prints, Nevie was honest about a bag we found in her closet. My gluten-free daughter was hoarding food in her bedroom, hiding it away from the rest of the family, but I was still a proud mama—not because of the dishonest act, but because of the courage she demonstrated in confessing what she had done. It was an indication that she was growing up in a home where she felt safe and secure, so much so that she was willing to unearth her secret in order to heal the places inside her heart that had been torn up by keeping it. Most kids have a similar conscience. They desire to be honest and to please their parents. They also desire to be known for who they truly are. Don't we all?

Nevie and I talked about how good it felt to confess her secret and to be seen in full light. I was tempted, naturally, to discipline her for "stealing" and "lying" and all the other wrong behaviors I could identify. However, because of God's grace and my play-therapy training, I was able to see past the behavior (thank You, Jesus) and allow God to use this opportunity to develop rich soil. I held my tongue and, instead, listened and reflected back her own conclusions about why she had done that and how it had made her heart feel. I affirmed Nevie's choice to trust me and divulge the secret; in so doing, something that the enemy would have used to twist my daughter's sense of confidence and integrity was instead used to nourish the soil of her heart.

As our CG group tackles middle school, we rely on the years of relationship we have built with one another and with Jesus. We have developed the kind of intimacy that only grows over long periods of time spent with Jesus and loving one another through the good, the bad and the smelly. We have had hard, uncomfortable conversations over the years but have emerged on the other side intact. This is why Courageous Girls groups need to be long-term. One year is not enough to see the depths of one another or to traverse through difficult situations without losing faith in one another's humanity. I want our daughters to know that no matter what they do or what has been done to them, God can use it all to make something beautiful! Embracing the holy crap in all our lives is how we remind ourselves that we are all experiencing the ongoing process of sanctification. Surrendering to Jesus is a learning process and requires a community in which we can learn and grow. Accepting that "poop" has a place and potential in God's economy reveals the strength and humility of a Courageous Girl.

Takeaway

What "poop" have you buried from your past? Revisit a past hurt or struggle for a moment. How did you overcome that? If there is still work to be done, make a commitment to find resources to help you: a local support group, a counselor, a trusted accountability partner, a good friend who has experienced something similar. Remember that being honest with yourself and another about the pain it caused is the first step in healing.

Take It a Step Further

Don't stop there. Get gut-wrenchingly real with yourself. How has your past hurt and pain seeped into your family's life? Specifically, how is it impacting your daughter? Is she showing signs of similar struggles or facing challenges that trigger your own past? What are you willing to start addressing today? If you are unsure, read through Isaiah 61 and pay attention to the words and phrases that stand out to you. Notice how God's greater redemption plan is moving from loss to restoration. Waiting for heaven or just hoping your daughter figures it out on her own is not enough. Ask God to guide you in helping your daughter become a mighty oak, rooted in God's Word and healing. Write these thoughts, emotions, and hopes down in your journal so that you will remember what God has done later in your life.

3

She Feels to Heal

There are few more viscerally transformational experiences than the secure embrace of a loving parent, especially when the child truly recognizes their need.

- **JAY WOLF**, *HOPE HEALS*

Blessed be the God and Father of our Lord Jesus Christ, the Father of compassion and the God of all comfort, who comforts us in all our troubles, so that we can comfort those in any trouble with the comfort we ourselves have received from God.

- **2 CORINTHIANS 1:3-4, NIV**

SHE EMBRACES THE RAINBOW OF EMOTIONS

I was twenty-five by the time I could acknowledge I had feelings. I recall my closest girlfriends confronting me in college for being overly optimistic. I was confused; I thought being positive was a godly attribute. I had only practiced "mind over matter" and chosen to find the silver lining in every situation. My parents instilled in me an ability to reframe my circumstances, a powerful skill I will discuss in later chapters. However, I did not know how to process negative emotions well. I viewed vulnerable emotions as excuses, signs of weakness, and obstacles to living the fullest life. Most of my mentors in the church had reinforced this perspective and affirmed my outlook in unintentional ways. However, as I ventured through my training as a clinician, I learned how failing to model healthy processing of negative feelings can cause children to cope in potentially damaging ways.

I learned to cope with negative emotions through an eating disorder called bulimia. As a curvy young girl growing up in a culture that idealized a thin frame, I did not let anyone know about my unpleasant feelings, like disappointment, insecurity, loneliness and discouragement. Instead of directly acknowledging and naming those feelings, I channeled the relief of such emotions into trying to control my body size. Like most parents, we follow the generational patterns of our family line unless we consciously choose to learn a different way. My parents made huge efforts to shift the legacy of their homes, and I am grateful for the ways I was able to navigate my struggles over time.

Regardless of our stories, if we do not address negative emotions with our children, we open their lives to a plethora of unhealthy coping mechanisms. Maladaptive behaviors related to controlling emotions might look like food restriction, weight tracking, overeating, binging, and compulsive exercising, or more pain-numbing behaviors like drinking, smoking, vaping, drug use, pornography use, sex, masturbation, self-harm, and a myriad of other challenges. Learning how to process every emotion that a girl feels is part of the journey of becoming courageous.

The United States is ranked as one of the world's most addicted and desensitized societies.[1] This reality, coupled with our culture's current state of numbing activities (acting on the desire to check out from reality) is not encouraging. There is little to inspire hope that things will improve across our nation. One of the reasons for this is that we do not have a cultural "norm" for grieving. We are not expected to move healthily through our God-designed emotions; we prefer fast-food type processing that makes us happy. We teach kids to "toughen up" or to "grin and bear it." We are coached to "fake it 'til we make it" and to "play through the pain." In church circles, we can even succumb to the idea that negative emotions are ungodly and train ourselves to focus on the "blessings." I have heard these same phrases taught to both boys and girls, though girls are hardwired with higher sensitivity to their environment and relational dynamics than boys. This fascinating difference in brain development is another reason why our daughters need help honoring their emotions.[2]

SHE RECOGNIZES DENIAL

Growing up I viewed myself as a "good girl," and so I hid my internal conflict. Rather than showing my struggles with risky external behaviors like drinking, using sex or angry outbursts to release emotional tension, I disconnected from my true heart and focused on performing well in school, sports, leadership, and body-image management. Since I was not processing with anyone else outside my own head, I developed many false narratives that I held deep inside. I know many girls can relate. I also know my parents never meant to teach me that it was wrong to express feelings; my family has discussed this openly in my adult years. However, we all have a tendency, especially in Christian circles, to ignore our feelings and push past them.

Our tendency to ignore our negative emotions might stem from our families' habits, or we might have practiced denial for so long that it feels normal. Some cultures suppress emotions more than others. Asian cultures are notorious for this tendency and leave individuals at high risk for developing unhealthy habits around emotional intelligence. Regardless of the ways we do this, all dysfunctional families convey, intentionally or unintentionally, these basic rules: (1) do not talk about anything meaningful, (2) do not trust others, and (3) do not allow yourself to feel your emotions. We transmit most of these lessons indirectly through patterns lived out in our ordinary daily lives.[3]

Our children catch what we live, not necessarily what we say. For example, when they hear a mom lying to a friend about why she cannot attend a gathering, this models that bending the truth is a clever way to avoid conflict. Or, a home without any conflict conveys that it's inappropriate to discuss feelings. Think about the wife who never tells her husband that he hurt her feelings. Imagine he scolded her for overextending her budget at the grocery store, but instead of communicating her hurt, she just turns to the dishes at the kitchen sink so that no one sees the tears silently streaming down her cheeks. The child living in this home may know her father acted unkindly but never learns from her mother how to handle his belittling behavior. If the mother suffers in silence and promptly becomes cheery at the next opportunity to transition about of her sadness, the moment is gone and so are the emotions that came with it.

Another common practice in denial is parents teaching children not to tell "family secrets." Children are programmed not to trust anyone outside of their family (despite dishonesty within the family) and to avoid sharing what may happen within the walls of the home. Not wanting to ruffle feathers or be seen as ungrateful, children alter how they might otherwise act or behave, especially in how they express themselves. These messages, embedded in young, impressionable brains, create deep neural pathways that impact children's development. Do any of these sound familiar to you? Can you identify any messages from the dysfunctional family system?

SHE REGULATES HER EMOTIONS

If you have received messages from a dysfunctional family system that practices denial, it's important to know that we can retrain ourselves to recognize and regulate our emotions. Even if we have grown up with a distorted view of negative emotions, we can learn to pay attention to what they tell us about our reality. For example, when we feel angry, we might notice our jaw tightens or our hands start to clench. This kind of body awareness helps a person learn their natural responses to the world around them. Sometimes a child might have a stomach ache when they are anxious. When we can identify the emotions, then we can help them calm down. This is called "self-regulating," a term counselors use to describe how to be aware of one's feelings and meet a human need in a legitimate way. If I could narrow down the one skill I have needed to teach in my counseling practice more than any other skill, it would be the ability to self-regulate. Before I explain how to develop this strength, I want to explain why *feeling* is so important.

Healthy brain development and spiritual formation require that we learn to process our feelings, especially when those feelings are more intense in nature. A myth, inadvertently taught by Christian families, is that faith is primarily related to what we *think* to be true. This rationale places primary importance on our frontal lobe (upper brain), which is responsible for decision-making and rational thoughts. This assumption undermines the way God created humans and the importance of our emotions, which reside in the amygdala (lower brain) and are carried out by the limbic or nervous system. Often, this form of mind over matter stresses that we must not "give into our emotions." This teaching comes from passages like Romans 12:2: "Renew your mind," and 2 Corinthians 10:5, "Take every thought captive and make it obedient to Christ." Undoubtedly, these are powerful scriptures, and we will address them in a later chapter. However, framing faith as a primarily thought-based exercise causes us to cast our emotions in a negative light. Ultimately, this causes us to compartmentalize our lives and prevents us from fully integrating all of who we are. The Lord wants *all* of us: mind, heart, body and actions. That includes our emotions. There are thirty-nine verses throughout the Bible that speak to loving God with our "whole heart." There are many more verses that encourage us to love God with *all* of who we are.

One of the most well-known verses says, "Love the Lord your God with all your heart, with all your soul, with all your mind, and with all your strength..." (Luke 10:27, NIV). When we experience disconnect between our mind, body and emotions, we need to pause and assess what's happening. When I was a new mom, I lost my work-out routine (for a good cause). However, without a way to regularly release stress, my irritation was flaring and my anxiety was rising. My body knew I would feel better if I could exercise a few times each week, but my mind kept telling me that I was a bad mom if I took time away from my daughters. My mind also told me that my lack of exercise was Jeff's fault because...well, there was no real reason, but I just needed someone to blame.

Taking time to pause and reflect, I listened to what was happening inside my body (anxiety), my emotions (irritation and bitterness), and my mind (a workout would help me, but good moms do not take time away from their babies to exercise). Doing so helped me work through the three warring parts of myself before the Lord. I decided to comfort my body and emotions by making an exercise plan. My mind soon learned that Jeff was not standing in my way, and my babies did fine without me for three hours a week. In fact, I was a better mom when I was with them because of my regular exercise. It is not healthy to lead only with our emotions, nor is it healthy to lead only with our logic. Loving God with all of who we are requires integrating our emotions with our minds and our bodies. So, how do we move in this direction?

Dr. Daniel Siegel, a leading neuroscientist and parenting expert, and Tina Payne Bryson, Ph.D, have helped the mental-health field understand how a person develops healthy decision-making, self-awareness, school success, relationships, and other important aspects that lead one to wellness and integration. The authors use a clever analogy of a two-story house, describing a child's brain as having both an upstairs and a downstairs. The downstairs brain, responsible for the lower-level functioning, is in charge of impulses, emotions, and basic life functions like breathing and blinking. The upstairs brain is responsible for mental processing—decision-making, morality, empathy, and self-awareness. The upstairs brain is constantly under construction until the age of twenty-four (did you catch that?); the downstairs brain is fully functional at birth.[4] Pause for a moment and let that sink in. Our children need a lot of patience and coaching throughout their growing years. If we were not coached in our childhood, we might need it too!

If we consider the brain, we see that from the beginning God created us as emotional beings with basic functionality who are primarily sensory-oriented. He did not give us the ability to fully engage our logical brains until the middle of our twenties, well into adulthood. This explains why I wasn't fully in touch with my own emotions until age 25! It should go without saying that a significant part of our job as parents is to support our children's emotional brain development. We are the helpers that integrate the two halves (emotional and rational) of our children's brains, and God was so gracious in giving us this role. It is mind blowing to realize that God designed us to map out our world through sensory and emotional attachments, long before we can make sense of the logical relationships that occur through linear decision-making. This is why we in Courageous Girls focus so much on emotional health and attunement (the ability to emotionally sense natural rhythms, patterns and connections within ourselves). We are able to "love because we were first loved" (1 John 4:7). Our children will not be able to love others well unless they first experience what it is like to be loved completely, big emotions and all!

Self-regulation occurs when we do something to calm ourselves down like go for a walk, breathe deeply, journal, listen to music, or exercise. As Dr. Siegel says, the most emotionally healthy people are those who know how to keep both their upstairs and downstairs engaged.[5] This does not come naturally but must be taught to our girls and modeled by us moms. Those who grew up in chaotic, emotionally neglectful, narcissistic, or abusive homes find self-regulating harder than most. The necessity to map out danger has given your brain a fast track to protect and react before it can assess safety. God created this automatic system to help us in danger; without it, we would be far more vulnerable in crisis. For example, this warning system helps a person quickly slam on their car breaks when abruptly approaching the red brake lights from a slowing car in front. This system is extremely helpful in the midst of real danger but damaging when it goes off too frequently or at unnecessary times.

Learning to self-regulate our emotional brains takes a lot of practice, safety, patience and self-awareness, especially if we have been accustomed to ignoring our bodies and feelings over many years. Here's a helpful process to walk you through the steps of being more emotionally aware as a mom:

1. Identify the emotion. (Name it as accurately as you can.)

2. Identify where the emotion is in the body (where are you feeling changes in your body?) and where the emotion registers on your emotional thermometer (on a scale of 0 to 10, with 10 being the most intense).

3. Identify the source, if possible. (What caused it?)

4. Identify what that particular emotion needs. (What would bring comfort or calm it down?)

5. Advocate for that need. (This can be a hard one to learn, but practice helps.)

I usually ask the following questions in a prayerful manner, and I encourage you to try the same before teaching your daughters to regulate their emotions. It might look something like this:

Lord, I am feeling something negative after Bible Study. What is that feeling?

Vulnerability.

Lord, where do I feel vulnerable in my body?
It's your gut. It feels restless, like churning.

What would You say is the source of it, Lord?
You want to be liked, and you didn't get any feedback from the group.

What does that vulnerability need?
You need someone to remind you that you are still loved and liked. You need to know that I still used what you were able to give today.

Where do I turn for that affirmation, Lord?
I can give that to you. You are always enough to me, Terra. You can also ask someone from your encouragement team to remind you of who you are as well.

My prayerful reflection usually ends like this:
Lord, help me to have courage to advocate for my needs and move into action. Show me, again, how You designed me and made me precious to You.

I might text a friend for encouragement or wait for the Lord to send some my way.

The result: usually peace. Sometimes it takes time.

Vulnerability is not my favorite emotion. (Can you tell?) You know the feeling: the one that creeps in right after you shared an embarrassing story or tried to offer wisdom in a room full of people you do not know well. You wonder what they think of you as they stare at you awkwardly with distant smiles. The truth is, you will never know what they really think. It feels like walking through town after forgetting to put on your clothes. I still dread that feeling when it comes, and yet I try to practice what I preach.

The most powerful teaching moments are the ones full of raw and real emotions—emotions we'd like to cover up with a gentle sniffle and polite smile but that really come out as heaving sobs and constant nasal drip. When we honor how we actually feel (versus how we think we *should* feel or *wish* we felt) and teach our daughters to do the same, we teach them that they matter. We impart to them a tangible truth that God meets them where they are and that they are important and worthy of our attention, care and concern. Every single person wants to know they are the apple of someone's eye. Walking your daughter through this exact process after a particularly challenging day at school or after a disappointing loss will not only help her identify and grow her own emotional awareness, but it will draw you closer together as she builds greater trust in your relationship.

I love King David and his psalms; they are full of passion, deep emotions and raw humanity. You can actually see David processing his emotions through song writing, journaling and prayer. In Psalm 17:8, David writes:

> I call on you, my God, for you will answer me;
> turn your ear to me and hear my prayer.
> Show me the wonders of your great love,
> you who save by your right hand
> those who take refuge in you from their foes.
> Keep me as the apple of your eye;
> hide me in the shadow of your wings
> from the wicked who are out to destroy me,
> from my mortal enemies who surround me.

You can hear the desperation in his cry as Saul and his army hunt for him. In his plea, I hear that David deeply trusts that God will answer his cry and turn toward him. Not only does David know God will hear him, He believes God will show him great demonstrations of love so that David can find refuge in Him. King David is a wonderful example of a person after God's heart, and yet he felt an extremely wide range of emotions.

SHE CAN IDENTIFY HER OWN FEELINGS AND CONNECT WITH THE EMOTIONS OF OTHERS

As I mentioned earlier, I once heard a leader preach from the pulpit that it is a sin to feel despair. This person believed that true faith in God means we should never be anxious or experience sadness because we should always find joy in all that we do. I am unconvinced this is biblical. In fact, I think there are so many verses around emotional regulation because God knows we have emotions and expects us to experience them. Being happy all the time, speeding through the concourse of life on the autopilot of joy, does not reflect the full image of God. God displays an array of emotions in scripture. The Bible tells us to "be content in all circumstances" and to "rejoice always," but those phrases are declarations, not commandments. In other words, "do not be anxious, but in prayer and petition" in Philippians 4:6 is a guide for when we *are* anxious, not a rebuke for experiencing anxiety.

When Lazarus died, Jesus wept with Mary and Martha. Jesus knew that He would soon raise Lazarus from the dead, but He joined these beloved women in pain even though He knew healing was coming. This is the example I want to exemplify for my daughters. If we can be Courageous Mamas who join our girls wherever they are on their emotional thermometer (even when we know the situation is not as critical as they may believe it is in the moment), they will have healthier brain development overall. This is empathy: an ability to see and feel someone else's experience whether you have experienced it or not. Girls will grow up to be healthier adults with a better chance at having healthier emotional relationships. Their memories will be more intact and the brain will store them with more clarity. And best of all, our daughters will have a greater chance of understanding and embodying the kind of love our God has and offers us.

When my youngest was a baby, she would nuzzle her nose into my armpit and sleep with her face surrounded by my arms. She was hiding in the shadow of my wings, finding rest and comfort. I want to live like this with God, and I want to teach my girls how to do the same. The process of teaching our daughters how to find refuge in times of anxiety, disappointment, anger, jealousy and other difficult emotions is a journey fostered by intentionally pursuing their hearts. The greatest chance for our girls to believe God meets them in real life is for them to experience that reality with those whom they trust the most: their moms. A Courageous Girl can name her emotions, she can identify and advocate for her needs, and she can find comforting peace in her relationship with God and other trusted people in her life.

Part of teaching our children empathy is paying attention to teaching moments when they arise. Unfortunately, it is easy to minimize or indirectly communicate to our kids that they do not matter by ignoring their emotions. This approach affects their ability to identify their emotions accurately and to empathize with others. We all do this, intentionally or otherwise, and as a trained professional counselor, I am no different. For example, if your daughter falls and bumps her knee, you might tell her to be a "big girl" or to "laugh it off." If you tell her "you are fine," or ignore her to mitigate her "drama queen tendencies," you also invalidate her experience. When your daughter says she does not want to go to school, you may say, "You don't have a choice," or "You have a pretty good life if the worst thing you have to do is go to school." When you tell her to "suck it up," you communicate that her problems do not matter.

A more subtle, but equally dangerous, response is when our children's pain evokes powerful emotions in us. If your daughter tells you that a friend said something mean to her, you may respond with your own "hurt" emotions. Your own outrage (how dare someone treat your daughter that way!) might provoke you to get mad at the friend, too. In this situation, your daughter must comfort you or minimize her pain in order to protect you. Instead of leaning into your daughter's emotional need, your emotions hijack the conversation and your anger becomes the focus. This is not empathy, though it may feel like it. An inability to regulate our emotions when our children are in pain communicates we cannot handle what they feel inside. The indirect message is: *Your emotions are too big for me! Therefore, you are on your own.* In essence, we tell our child to suppress her feelings since we are not ready, capable or willing to address them with her. Because parents are the first depiction of who God is, our actions can convey that God is not strong enough to handle our feelings. When this is communicated, children learn to hold back their emotions from their families and from God.

These are all things that relatively healthy parents do; there is no shame in admitting to these moments. I know how deeply these actions impact my kids, and even I still do it! Therein lies our need for grace. As moms, we cannot hear this word enough. We *must* extend grace, to ourselves, and to our girls growing in their own courage and strength. Our daughters are looking to us to teach them how to move through and regulate emotions, not to avoid and move around them.

SHE LISTENS WELL

One of the easiest ways to practice grace with our children is to grow in the discipline of listening. Learning to empathize with our daughters not only helps them calm their brains and build trust, but it also teaches them how to empathize with others. We cannot give away what we have not received. There are lots of ways experts teach how to listen well. For the sake of simplicity, here are three effective and essential ingredients to being a good listener: mirroring, validating, and empathizing.

Mirroring is literally reflecting back what a person is saying. This is not a time for interpretation and there are no questions asked until the person is completely done sharing. Often times, questions can dominate and control a conversation and will shut down the other person before we ever hear the whole story. Clarifying questions can be asked after the speaker has shared all she wants to share. This might determine what questions you actually ask in the end. Mirroring might look like this:

Addie: "Mom, I was frustrated and embarrassed today when you said I hadn't cleaned my room in front of my friend."

Me (in an authentic and caring tone): "It did not feel good to you when I pointed out that you did not clean your room in front of your friend."

Addie: "Yes! Exactly."

Me: "Are you finished or do you have more to share with me?"

Addie: "No, that is it."

Me: "Can I ask a clarifying question now?"

Addie: "Sure."

Me: "What would you suggest I do differently next time?"

Addie: "It would have been nice if you waited until after we got home, when it was just us, to tell me about my room."

The benefit of mirroring is that we are able to slow our reaction down by listening before we respond. In doing so, we are more likely to hear exactly what the speaker is saying. When we listen to others, we often form a response in our mind while the other person is still talking and miss what they are saying. When this happens, we are not truly listening. We may only hear a few words because we are more focused on our rebuttal. This approach makes us more likely to respond defensively, with incomplete information or insufficient understanding. When our children speak, it is imperative that we are present and fully focused. We need to hear our daughter's experiences in their entirety so that we, as the more experienced adult, can pay attention to her nonverbal communication—body language, tone of voice, heavy sighs, avoidance of eye contact, etc. These details can give us strong clues on our child's emotional state.

Finally, we understand the importance of mirroring from a neurological perspective. The Creator designed our brains in a magnificent way. Did you know that the part of the brain that processes our auditory input is separate from the part that processes our verbal output? In other words, we hear from a different part of the brain than where we speak. Our daughters process their words differently by hearing those same words repeated back to them. So often we think we are communicating clearly until we hear our words repeated back to us. When our daughter says, "No, that is not what I mean!" we can simply keep mirroring until she recognizes the message she is trying to get across. A powerful implication is that the speaker, in this case our daughter, will feel her body start to calm down, and she will make better sense of her own world. Mirroring helps a girl learn what she thinks, feels, and how she articulates that to those around her—a vital relational skill for every area of life.

Validating occurs when we put on someone else's lens and cognitively understand their perspective. Validating does not require agreement and often takes humility to be able to see someone else's viewpoint. Validating is a nonjudgmental approach that meets a person where they are. It's a crucial ingredient in learning to listen well, especially when we might be tempted to think that the other person (our child, perhaps) has an inaccurate or incomplete perspective. Validation is a way of showing respect and acknowledging that another's point of view is valid *to them*. It's also a way to recognize, "If I was in their shoes, I might come to the same conclusion they reached." Here is an example of a response to the same conversation outlined above that does *not* validate my daughter's feelings:

Addie: "It would have been nice if you waited until after we got home, when it was just us, to tell me about my room."

Me: "Well, if you hadn't waited for six days to clean your room, we wouldn't have had the discussion at all!"

Not only does a response like this invalidate Addie by refusing to see her perspective at all, but it places her in the shadow of shame by pointing out to what degree she failed. It's like rubbing salt in an already open wound. Most of us do not respond well to invalidation (this is true for all humans), yet we do not recognize when we are doing it to others. We are often repeat offenders of invalidation, especially in our own homes.

Let's look at how I could have responded to Addie in a more validating way:

Addie: "It would have been nice if you waited until after we got home, when it was just us, to tell me about my room."

Me: "I can see how you might have felt embarrassed and why you would have wanted me to wait to talk to you. It sounds like you are not upset that I talked to you about your messy room, but that I did it in front of your friend. That makes a lot of sense. I didn't need to do that. There was plenty of time after we dropped your friend off to discuss the issue."

Empathizing is the final, and often missed, step in effective listening. It is less about the cerebral understanding and more about the emotion. This is where human attachment, connection and comfort grow, because in empathy we receive the message "I am not alone." Empathizing looks like this:

Me: "Addie, it seems you feel frustrated, embarrassed, and maybe even disappointed that I would say this in front of your friend. Is that true?"

Addie: She nods yes and I can see her shoulders relax in relief.

Giving your daughter a chance to reply and tell you more is always a good thing. In fact, you might guess the wrong emotions and, in grace, she can tell you what her feelings actually are. The point is to join her where she is at and not to expect her to understand or possess an adult perspective. If there is a discipline or a lesson to be learned, you can ask your daughter *after* she has been fully heard: "Are you willing to hear where I was coming from?" She might say no and you can respect that, but say, "I will give you thirty minutes, and then we can talk." Most likely if you heard her well, she will be more open to hearing you.

Empathizing with our daughters teaches them how to receive and offer empathy. This requires lots of coaching, but through trial and error, you will both improve at this skill. In time, it will serve you well in all of your relationships. Neuroscientists have mapped out a person's brain when they are experiencing empathy with another; there is literally increased blood flow throughout various regions in the brain, which creates a calming effect. Ultimately, this de-escalates strong emotions and prevents the thermometer from rising even higher on the ten-point scale so that we can engage our world with both the upstairs and downstairs brains.

Both moms and daughters may find themselves needing these tools. Whether you are in need of them now or find yourself desperate for ways to connect with your daughter, active and effective listening is a practical and easy place to start. The end of the day or bedtime can provide for some space to listen. Slow down and take the opportunity in typical day-to-day moments to be present enough to attune to your daughter's feelings. Comfort is a God-designed human need, and we want to teach our children this vital skill before they move through the difficult pain that lurks outside the safety of home. By experiencing healthy relationships in the home, our daughters have a better chance to choose healthier relationships as teens and adults. They will also become a safe place where others can land. The goal is to give our daughters lots of practice while they are young—choosing to be honest, talking about their feelings, asking for what they need, responding appropriately when there is a no or a negative response, etc. In turn, we develop healthier brains for our girls and for ourselves! God is so clever.

SHE IS INTENTIONAL AND COMFORTS

One of the gifts of gathering together as Courageous Girls groups is having the regular routine and accountability to turn toward, talk to, and listen to your daughter at least once a month. That may sound absurd (aren't we listening to them all the time?!), but practicing authentic communication that actively stimulates heart connection and increases emotional regulation is different than the daily rantings and run-downs. It requires intentionality and a desire to sit in her reality with her. This can be hard with the ever-increasing pace of life we all keep. It is even less likely to happen if we are constantly being drawn away by the ding of an incoming text message or the whistle of a Facebook message. But intentionality is the bedrock of becoming courageous, and so we must practice this as mothers with our children, as wives in our marriages, and as confidantes in our friendships.

The rhythm of the Courageous Girls discussion format fosters open relationships between moms and daughters, creating safe spaces where girls feel heard, known and accepted. One of the moms in my group waited patiently for four years before her daughter began to share deeply with her. For years she built a foundation of trust but wondered why her daughter did not share much, especially at an emotional level. She just seemed uninterested or guarded. Then one day, after a hard day at school, they had the most touching moment. In that week, the mother realized God had been preparing her to listen when her daughter needed her the most. We celebrated together because this signaled a turning point in their relationship.

We may not see these investments in our daughters in everyday patterns of life. However, creating an open posture toward our children where intimacy and vulnerability are embraced and encouraged will pay off in the end. More importantly, it will give them tangible experiences of what these traits look like with God and others. How awesome it is when healthy relationships are practiced at home before it becomes necessary to model them as adults! Normalizing these processes early in their lives will help our daughters move through the teen and college years well.

At times, it may seem impossible for moms to know how to comfort their daughters unless they received this training in their own childhood homes or experienced healthy relationships in adulthood. Learning how to comfort begins with tuning in to our own emotions. In fact, much of the trauma recovery process in professional counseling settings aims first to help people feel and then teaches them how to receive comfort from others. When we experience abuse or neglect, we are conditioned to believe that what we think, feel, need or want *does not* and *should not* matter. It can take a woman many years to recover from the devastation of violation, so having grace for ourselves in the healing process is critical. In pursuing a deeply intentional relational journey with your daughter, you are already moving boldly and courageously toward healing and wholeness for yourself as well.

Growing up, I could rationalize any emotion I felt to the extent that it temporarily disappeared. Some of that is related to how I am wired. I successfully pushed past any feelings that tried to move into my reality. My skills to reframe difficulties served me well at times. I cautiously refer to this as the "athlete mentality"—*no pain, no gain.* There are some significant benefits to the athlete mentality that look like resilience and determination. Playing sports often teaches children how to commit to something they start, which positively impacts future relationships and endeavors. Sports also help us learn the difference between discomfort and true injury, an important life skill. The danger presents itself when we ignore true injuries and live in denial, choosing to bury pain rather than regularly offering it back to God (and in many cases get professional help). Throughout my education, I played sports with injuries, all the while ignoring the pain in my body. I fell in love with volleyball and spent many years competing on a knee injury until I had no other choice but to have my entire ACL repaired - ending my Olympic volleyball career track. (Okay, maybe just my high school career, but do not minimize the loss!)

There is a clear correlation between learning to ignore physical pain in the body and ignoring emotional or psychological pain.[6] Knowing how to identify and process our emotions and knowing how to connect with our bodies are intertwined; they are also connected to fully embracing our need for God. If we were made to tough it out on our own, why would we ever rely on help from our Creator or community? This is why emotional distress can literally make a person physically ill or cause long-term harm to the body. In the words of Shauna Niequist, author and speaker, "Many Christians, women especially, were raised to be obedient and easy, to swallow feelings, to choke down tears. This has not served us well. This has made it far too easy to injure our bodies and our souls in the name of good causes."[7] *Amen, sister.*

When I was younger, I learned to manage my anger, fear and disappointment by escaping through food, binging, purging and compulsively exercising. I stumbled into this maladaptive coping strategy as a way to illegitimately comfort uncomfortable feelings. I used to say that "Ben and Jerry" were some of my best friends, especially in the form of "Chunky Monkey." I have always had friends; I just didn't let them see me struggle. I had a deep, unmet need to be heard and had not learned how to really talk with my friends, cry, or acknowledge anger. Instead, my body would feel anxiety and I would automatically reach for food or go for a really long run. It was overwhelming and, at times, all-consuming. Regardless of natural-born wiring and personality, I see the same pattern in many girls and women who have not been taught how to honor their emotions. Controlling or being consumed by food, such as rigid rule keeping or living life for the next meal, are more subtle controlling behaviors that provide a momentary quick fix through a hormone called dopamine. These behaviors, and those of a similar nature, create bondage and are often followed by crippling shame.[8]

Thankfully, in high school I learned to cope with my emotions through journaling. Journaling has been found to be helpful for all kinds of recovery work. In some ways, it has given me at least one healthy outlet, albeit a secretive one, for all the emotions I felt throughout my teen years. As an adult who has spent years healing with God, I can look back over scribbled notes documenting my emotions and see the disconnect between my inner and outer worlds. I have learned so much more about who I am and my basic human needs through this practice, and I know I am not alone. The cry to be heard and find comfort is repeated in my office from every girl, teen, and woman who has ever been in touch with her heart. The amazing news is that comfort can be provided in many forms. However, one of the most satisfying and relief-producing ways to receive comfort is through the arms of a loving mother who accepts her daughter as she is and provides a steadfast strength reminding her all will be okay.

SHE RUNS TOWARD EMOTIONS, NOT AWAY

Courageous Girls—moms and daughters—practice engaging their emotions regularly. They learn how to handle their emotions, and those of others, with care. They regard one another with tenderness and utilize healthy coping strategies. If we learn how to process and regulate our emotions in appropriate ways, especially in the safety of our homes as we grow up, we will meet our God-given emotional needs in legitimate ways. If we do not learn this skill, we will leak emotional waste and try to meet our needs in illegitimate ways. At the core, most maladaptive behaviors are a desperate cry for empathy and compassion. This is why the key component of Courageous Girls is community. We need each other on every level. We need to learn to identify our needs at every point on the continuum, and we do this by listening to and learning from the experiences of others.

In a special way, Courageous Girls are mirrors for each other. Over time, and with healthy adult models who are willing to walk through these practices repeatedly, each girl can learn to regulate her emotions in productive and safe ways. All children need this support; truthfully, many adults do, too. Regulating emotions is so difficult, especially when we have not been taught to recognize or voice them.

Emotions are like trains; they move quickly. That is why they are called eMOTIONS—you can bank on the fact that there will be movement and constant flux. Some days they will be in check; other days they will veer off track. They may even run you over on occasion! We need to remember that emotions do not control us, but they help guide us to a more authentic self and connection with God and others. We need to grasp the depths of our sorrows in order to feel the height of our joy.

Unlike emotions, the love of God is constant. It is unmovable and never-changing, regardless of how we feel in the moment. We need to know how to ask for help, especially from a loving God; accepting our need for a Savior is the very foundation of our faith. When we have trouble regulating our emotions, we can turn to God and remember:

The LORD your God is with you, the Mighty Warrior who saves. He will take great delight in you; in His love He will no longer rebuke you, but will rejoice over you with singing (Zephaniah 3:17).

Takeaway

Journaling is one way to learn or relearn how to identify, express and share your emotions. Open a blank notebook and begin on page one. For many of us, knowing what to write about is the toughest part. Try this: Sit quietly with God for 10 minutes. Don't do, say or read anything. Just pay attention. Notice your thoughts. What thoughts or scenes are moving through your mind? Notice your body. What part of the body is more tense? Notice your environment. What do you see, smell, hear, taste, feel? Then read Psalm 139:23-24 and ask God to search you, help you see if there are any anxieties of which you are unaware, and write down impressions that come to mind. Then recognize that you are not alone in what you are carrying and ask God to lead you toward comfort.

Take It a Step Further

Start a mother/daughter journal, too. Share things with one another when you need or want. After writing a message or note, leave the journal back on your daughter's bed for her to read in her own time. Let her know that she can do the same, leaving her thoughts for you on your bed, too. Allow this tool to be a way to communicate on a deeper level, especially if tough conversations are new or haven't gone well in the past. There is safety in writing down our feelings before we give voice to them out loud. Practice doing this together and watch your relationship flourish.

4

She Tunes in to the Voice of Grace

What if I saw myself the way you see me? You are loved, not because of what you have done. Even when your heart has run the other way, nothing is going to change. He chose you. He sees you. He knows you. You are covered, Daughter.

- ELLIE HOLCOMB

That you may love the Lord your God, listen to His voice, and hold fast to Him.

- DEUTERONOMY 30:20

SHE KNOWS HER VALUE

C. S. Lewis once said, "I believe in Christianity as I believe that the sun will rise—not only because I see it, but because by it, I see everything else." What lens do you look through? Many women think their value is found in their appearance, performance, or good choices. The voices that say "I will never be good enough, smart enough, or pretty enough" haunt them. Some feel like they have to hide their true selves because if others really knew them, they would be rejected. If we are honest, to some extent we all try to be what our husbands want, parents dreamed of, or church communicates we should be. When we do this, anxiety rages. Our hearts are pulled in every direction, and we are left wanting to shut down or run away from others' expectations and needs. It is just a matter of time before we burn out.

We can all relate to burnout at some point in our story. Maybe you are the stay-at-home mom who dreamed of doing something mighty for Jesus' kingdom but feel worn and used up. Maybe you are now retired and look back on your life with nothing but despair, exhaustion, and cynicism. Or maybe you are the single thirty-year-old who finds herself feeling like she's an outsider to the "family" club at church. You might even be the pastor's wife or ministry leader who can help everyone else out of a crisis but you have no one to help you. Each of these situations reveals not only burnout but the realities of women who have focused on the expectations of others rather than on God's purpose for their lives. Expectations whisper from every part of society and, unless we silence them in our lives, they will not be quiet. Teaching our daughters how to discern the voice of the one true God starts with modeling how to evaluate whose voice is truly worthy.

One day, my oldest child asked me why I chose to be a counselor and inquired if I enjoy going to work. At the time, all I could say was that I am so honored to be a part of God's miracles through the transformation of people's lives. In my practice, I have heard woman after woman share their experiences with moms who were either ill-equipped to coach their daughters to listen to God's voice or, on the other hand, perpetuated lies to their daughters with loud and cruel spoken words. One woman shared that it has taken her forty years to replace her mom's voice with the voice of God, simply because her "Christian" mom confused and abused her so deeply. I hear stories of dads who could not be brave enough to risk inadequacy to pursue their daughter's heart and lacked tenderness, presence, and leadership. As a professional counselor, I have the opportunity to be a part of mending broken hearts and watching people experience God's life-changing love. In the end, my career has taught me how to love my girls well. I responded to my daughter's question, "Yes, I love going to work, but even more, I love being your mom." I want to live unencumbered by the voices of others and model that freedom in Christ to my children. Jesus is the only voice that is able to give us what we desperately need.

One of my favorite biblical narratives tells an account of a misunderstood individual known as the Samaritan woman. As a woman who had been married five times, I assume her situation provided rich content for local gossip. Even today, there are various commentaries around her situation: did she have so many husbands because she was adulterous or widowed? Regardless, I can imagine the burdens she carried. Surely surrounded by the unhelpful voices of others, she kept her head down in shame.

The Samaritan woman frequented a well outside the city to fetch water every day. Given the hostilities between Jews and Samaritans at that time, we can be certain that this was a well visited only by the Samaritan people. But one day, Jesus, a Jewish traveler, boldly made His way to the well. In doing so, Jesus defied many cultural norms of His day. Samaritan women were viewed as lowly as rabid dogs by some members of the community, but Jesus did not care. Even though she was a woman and a Samaritan, He looked her in the eye and conversed with her. I wonder if the Samaritan woman could look Jesus in the eye as she grappled with all the voices of guilt, shame and dishonor she had heard over the years.

During His conversation with her, Jesus asks the Samaritan woman for a drink of water. Cryptically, He tells her that if she knew the gift of God who asked her for a drink at the well, she would have asked Him for living water that would cause her to thirst no more. Naturally, the woman is intrigued. The ensuing conversation reveals that Jesus knows the woman is cohabiting with a man to whom she is not married, a disgraceful move for her time. But Jesus sees past her actions and into her heart. Seeing that she was searching for more but with no hope to find it, He tells her that He can give her what she needs. His voice, the truth, leads her to fulfillment. The story ends with the woman returning to her village to tell the whole town about her afternoon with Jesus. From her encounter, the Bible tells us that many more came to believe Jesus was the Messiah because of her boldness and courage (see John 4:4-42).

Like the Samaritan woman, we are all trying to quench our deepest thirsts through the voices of others. We live in the world where the prince of lies roars like a lion to find his next prey. He uses all the "cultural norms," the tragedies in our lives, and the narratives in our heads to try to drown out the voice of love. It does not take much to get us off track from the truth of God's grace and hope for our lives. The lies, or shame messages, can consume us. Courageous Girls helps mothers and daughters discern the difference between what God says and what the world and its prince subtly communicate. A Courageous Girl can discern God's voice.

SHE KNOWS HER SHEPHERD'S VOICE

Often, it can seem like hearing God's voice is reserved for spiritual giants. For some, it may feel too mystical or charismatic. But having a personal relationship with God means communicating with Him. I cannot imagine feeling close to my husband if we never even spoke, or if I did all the talking. (That may happen on occasion, but not on a regular basis.) According to God's Word and the experience of many of His children, we have a direct line to Him. You may be wondering if He only speaks in an audible voice. Not necessarily. God speaks through The Bible, our community, creation, our intuitions, and more. I think that the way we hear God is directly linked to our wiring. Learning our unique communication style with God is part of the maturing experience within intimacy. Hearing does not always mean we understand what God is saying, but recognizing and attuning to His voice are the starting points. Let's use the analogy of a baby in a mama's womb to better understand the power of tuning in to God's voice among all the world's noise. *Parents Magazine* shared this information in an article on their website:

> Doctors assumed that babies were born without any knowledge about the outside world. But recent research is questioning this assumption, offering clues to what babies comprehend in utero. They are able to research what they remember after they're born and how that information prepares them for the

world outside the womb. The uterus isn't exactly the quietest place to hang out. Not only can a baby hear the sounds of his mom's body—her stomach growling, her heart beating, the occasional hiccup or burp—but she can also hear noises from beyond…Of course, not all sounds are the same. Perhaps the most significant one a baby hears in utero is his mother's voice. Around the seventh and eighth month, a fetus's heart rate slows down slightly whenever his mother is speaking, indicating that mom's voice has a calming effect.[1]

What would it be like to be so close and intimate with our Creator that, like babies in the womb, what we hear in His presence prepares us for the outside world? Not only might we learn to pause when we hear Him speaking, allowing the calming effect of His truth to pierce our anxious ways, but we might also be able to discern His voice above all the other noises around us. And there is a lot of noise!

Tuning out the voices in our head and in the world around us is one of the most profound disciplines in the Christian walk. It changes everything, especially our perspective. Thanks to my systems training as a marriage and family therapist and the reframing skills my parents instilled in me, I have a natural inclination to pause and consider the context of any thought, experience, or message. Our basic beliefs about God, ourselves, and the purpose of this life shape all our decisions and choices today. Our views are birthed out of our cultural experiences, combined with our unique wiring, and we all must hold them up to what God says. The woman who practices using the Word of God as her lens has a firm foundation. There is no stopping that Courageous Girl!

In The Message version of John 10:1-16, it says:

Let me set this before you as plainly as I can. If a person climbs over or through the fence of a sheep pen instead of going through the gate, you know he's up to no good—a sheep rustler! The shepherd walks right up to the gate. The gatekeeper opens the gate to him and the sheep recognize his voice. He calls his own sheep by name and leads them out. When he gets them all out, he leads them and they follow because they are familiar with his voice. They won't follow a stranger's voice but will scatter because they aren't used to the sound of it.

Jesus told this simple story, but they had no idea what he was talking about. So he tried again. "I'll be explicit, then. I am the Gate for the sheep. All those others are up to no good—sheep stealers, every one of them. But the sheep didn't listen to them. I am the Gate. Anyone who goes through me will be cared for—will freely go in and out, and find pasture. A thief is only there to steal and kill and destroy. I came so they can have real and eternal life, more and better life than they ever dreamed of.

I am the Good Shepherd. The Good Shepherd puts the sheep before himself, sacrifices himself if necessary. A hired man is not a real shepherd. The sheep mean nothing to him. He sees a wolf come and runs for it, leaving the sheep to be ravaged and scattered by the wolf. He's only in it for the money. The sheep don't matter to him.

I am the Good Shepherd. I know my own sheep and my own sheep know me. In the same way, the Father knows me and I know the Father. I put the sheep before myself, sacrificing myself if necessary. You need to know that I have other sheep in addition to those in this pen. I need to gather and bring them, too. They'll also recognize my voice. Then it will be one flock, one Shepherd.

There is so much profundity in this passage. Jesus calls Himself a Good Shepherd, which locals would have understood as a comparison to being a sheep herder. In Jesus' day, shepherds would often name their sheep and could easily distinguish between the many in their flock. What's more amazing, sheep could discern their shepherd's call even if they were mingling with other herds. This is a powerful analogy as Jesus distinguishes Himself from the Pharisees and declares that He is the Gate. In this analogy, Jesus claimed He was the *only* way to eternal and abundant life. Unlike the enemy, who comes to kill, steal, and destroy (see John 10:10), Jesus came to give life abundant. The only power the enemy really has is to distract Jesus' followers from His voice by sending wolves into the sheep's pen.

The "voices" we hear in our heads are beliefs or schemas we develop from our life experiences and the influences around us. For example, if I trip over a curb, the voice in my head might tell me "you are so clumsy," or I might just laugh at myself and move on. The narrative is highly based on whose opinion I rely. Everyone develops these thinking patterns, even though we are not fully conscious of them or know how they develop. Sometimes the voices in our heads are simple misinterpretations, but sometimes they are restatements from influential people. In moments of difficulty, those we trust the most can have greater influence on how we interpret life experiences. When those relationships are positive, they can help align us to grace. But when they're negative, the effects can be devastating. For example, a coach who tells your daughter, "You will never be good enough," and fails to reinforce her other strengths, can have negative long-term effects on her psyche. Being the kind of mother who walks alongside her daughter and helps her discern God's voice is enormously vital to her long-term healing. This is when we have to help our daughters evaluate whose voice is the loudest: the coach's voice or God's?

One of our main jobs as parents is to help our daughters discern the voice of God and create space for them to hear His voice repeatedly so that, like a baby in the womb, they can recognize it quickly. "Quiet time," though an over-utilized, Christian-centric phrase, is still a crucial spiritual discipline. When we recognize why we need to tune in to the Word of God, the muscle that helps us discern God's voice from the world grows stronger. Modeling this rhythm and practicing it with our daughters help her build sustainable habits and live out of the greatness of God's love for her.

I once heard the analogy of being like a pickle. A pickle is a cucumber that has been marinated in brine for 24 hours. Dipping a cucumber in brine once a week will not create a pickle. Similarly, being in the Word once a week will hardly transform us. Creating healthy habits that are woven into the DNA of our Courageous Girls comes with recognition that it takes 10,000 hours to become an expert in something.[2] According to leadership expert Malcolm Gladwell, it's the magic number for those who achieve greatness in their field. What could happen if we applied this statistic to our time in the Word? We have to submerge ourselves wholly until we see the world through a biblical lens. Marinate, ladies. There is nothing like a juicy dill pickle!

Pastor Bill Thralls says, "What we believe about ourselves is a direct correlation of what we believe about our God."[3] Former theology professor Dr. Kerri Dearborn, at Seattle Pacific University, adds, "And what we believe about our God, tells us more about what we believe about ourselves."[4] Both are true. Our views of God and ourselves inform the way we live and the choices we make. Our beliefs impact how we act, and therefore inform how we feel. Remember how I said in chapter 3 that if we overemphasize our thoughts we can dishonor our emotions? Once we acknowledge that emotions are a part of experiencing the fullness of God and are not meant to be dismissed, we can reunite our belief system with the skill of leading our behaviors and our emotions. When these three are aligned, we develop integrity, which shrinks the gap between who we profess ourselves to be and how we live our lives. This takes great intentionality and awareness. Romans 12:1 says, "Therefore, I urge you, brothers and sisters, in view of God's mercy, to offer your bodies as a living sacrifice, holy and pleasing to God—this is your true and proper worship. Do not conform to the pattern of this world, but be transformed by the renewing of your mind. Then you will be able to test and approve what God's will is—his good, pleasing and perfect will." I urge you, sister, in view of God's mercy, let's give all of who we are to God—our emotions, our bodies, *and* our minds. We are a confused flock in need of a Shepherd.

Have you ever heard yourself or another say, "My heart is telling me one thing, but my mind is saying another"? We can feel pulled in different directions even within ourselves. God's Word is the leader and our mind is the one who sends the marching orders to the rest of our being. We can help our bodies and emotions catch up to where our minds meditate on God's truth. The Bible says, "We demolish arguments and every pretension that sets itself up against the knowledge of God, and we take captive every thought to make it obedient to Christ" (2 Corinthians 10:5, NIV). Neuroscience research only validates what the scriptures have been instructing us to do all along. Ashley Turner of the Huffington Post writes, "Meditation is perhaps the most crucial instrument to harness the power of thought, cultivate more peace, clarity and happiness. Learning to train the brain and focus our attention is crucial to thriving and cultivating a peak performance in any endeavor. Long-time psychotherapist Dr. Ron Alexander, speaks of MIND STRENGTH, or the resilience, efficacy and emotional intelligence that arise as we begin the process of controlling the mind. Mind strength is one of the most empowering tools we can employ to impact and improve all aspects of life."[5] This is not a new concept, though the research behind it is recent.

For thousands of years, Christians have been meditating. Meditation simply means to contemplate or reflect upon something. The key difference between Christian meditation and other forms of spiritual meditation is that the first has us fill our minds with Christ and the latter has us empty out our minds. Philippians 4:8 says, "Finally, (courageous mama), whatever is true, whatever is honorable, whatever is right, whatever is pure, whatever is lovely, whatever is of good repute, if there is any excellence and if anything worthy of praise, dwell on these things." The apostle Paul goes on to say in verse 9, "Whatever you learned or received or heard from me, put it into practice. And the God of peace will be with you." Can we imagine being so completely soaked in God's presence that we can tell our daughters to copy us? This is a sobering thought.

To summarize, science is proving that the power of meditation means taking space between thoughts and actions.[6] For centuries, Christians have been reading God's Word, memorizing scripture, and meditating on its wisdom to navigate life. The very core of our purpose in parenting is to tell our children who God is and who they are according to His Words. This is why we read our Bibles—to curl up in the arms of our Father like a newborn baby and listen to His voice apart from all the others.

You know the voices that compete with God's. Facebook. Instagram. Netflix. Superstars. Church. Christian stars. Girlfriends. Spouses. Family. Teachers. Bullies. Bosses. The list goes on. Attuning to God's voice takes time and diligence, and it's a primary goal of raising a daughter rooted in grace. God's voice is not critical, judgmental, harsh, or controlling. It's also not wholly permissive, dissociated or ambivalent. Instead, it's a voice full of love: "Never stopping, never ending, never giving up, unbreaking, always and forever love."[7] A Courageous Girl is able to hear this voice of love and through it discern what is true about God, herself and those around her.

SHE LETS GOD LIFT HER HEAD UP

For years, when I looked into the mirror, I thought I was ugly. Though I moved past the behaviors of bulimia once I confessed to my parents, the thought patterns around my appearance still haunted me. My journey toward healing has helped me empathize with so many over the years. Looking back, I remember the struggle of waking up in the morning; my first thought, "I am ugly," informed how I prepared for the day. I would fixate on what I should wear, how to style my hair, or how to apply my makeup. I was completely consumed by my outer appearance. Some days, I would throw my hands in the air and give up, putting on a hat, sweats, and a baggy sweatshirt instead. In either case, I was unable to enjoy the gifts throughout my day as I meditated on my appearance.

In college, I decided to take the challenge of a professor on campus. I posted a sticky note on my dorm mirror that said, "I am fearfully and wonderfully made" (Psalm 139:14). For 90 days straight, I read that verse out loud and purposed to take my thoughts captive. In that 90-day period, God began to change my beliefs. I recall the morning when I stood before the mirror and the thought "I am beautiful" popped into my head. It was not a vain, conceited thought, but it was like I heard and agreed with the Father as He delighted in my appearance. That moment changed the rest of my actions that day and in the weeks following. I took less time to get ready in the mornings, while still valuing my body by showering and making myself presentable. The time it took to get ready decreased, and my focus on others increased. I was no longer engulfed in my thoughts, and I began to truly embrace His voice spoken in Psalm 139. The odd thing is that no one ever told me I was ugly. In fact, quite the opposite. There was no human that could quench the desire of my heart to be beautiful. Instead, I needed to experience the Father gently lifting my head, speaking His truth over me.

Danger lurks in the places where we make our identity into something other than what God intended. If we do not know the Word well, we can go to others who have walked with God a little longer and can help us discern His ways. A Bible study can help us grow. Meeting with other Courageous Mamas or mentors can help, too. Doing a devotional with our daughters is beneficial to both mom and daughter. And, of course, prayer can be a powerful way to discern God's voice. Get into the habit of asking Him to show you if something is of Him or of the world. He is faithful to answer.

SHE RECOGNIZES GRACE OVER PERFORMANCE

The very essence of our faith is that we are loved. You are loved. Your daughter is loved. I have spent many years trying to earn love by being the best daughter, wife, leader, mom, friend, speaker and counselor. I am done with that way of being, and I invite you to be done as well. I have officially declared that I no longer need to earn anyone's love, because God says so. He took care of everything we would ever need on the cross. If I try to earn His grace by measuring up to some else's expectation, I exhaust valuable energy that I could be using to show grace to others. Trying to prove ourselves worthy of love is a clever tactic the enemy uses to keep us ineffective. As we wake up to a new day every morning, God proves that He is for us. His grace is undeserved favor. Our job is to plug ourselves into relationship and let Him do the rest!

The very essence of the Christian faith is that "by grace you have been saved" (Ephesians 2:5b). The definition never ceases to amaze me as I pause and remember the kindness of God. It is because of grace, not my own efforts, that I have been pursued, chosen, and redeemed. Before I understood the power of grace, I was tormented by pleasing others. I was caught in the trap of performance-based Christianity—much like the sticker trap in Max Lucado's book. I tried so hard to be all I could be—but for the sake of what? I still do not know, but I see the same messages permeating every woman around me. Once in a while, I find a "Lucia" who stands out, and I can discern the grace surrounding her. She has tasted and seen that the Lord is good and can be trusted.

The word "grace" (*chen* in Hebrew, *charis* in Greek) literally means "favor." In our case, it means "undeserved favor."[8] God stoops down toward us because He is love and kindness; He makes a way for us to be loved, known, and accepted. Though I began my relationship with Christ as a young girl, I did not understand "saved by grace" until my twenties. Somehow, between my upbringing, my wiring, and the Christian teachings in my circles, I learned to be a good Christian by *striving* to be like Jesus, instead of allowing God to conform me into His image. If you have been in the church for a while, you might struggle with that statement. However, the enemy is like a wolf in sheep's clothing. He takes a truth in God's Word and, with a little manipulation, twists it into something God never intended. Similar to steering a ship, the slightest change in coordinates will create a major shift in the ship's course and, ultimately, its destination.

As mamas raising daughters we dearly love, we might give into the voice that says we should raise respectful, obedient, polite girls who know their Bible and "make good choices." Or, on the other side, you might be drawn to the messages "Be you" and "Who cares what anyone else thinks. You are enough." Even the Disney message "Trust your heart" sounds good. The younger church blends the two messages, and we are really confused now! We must think critically, "Is this what Jesus really meant when He saved us by grace alone? And how do I teach truth to my daughters so that they will not be caught in the same traps?" Remember these truths: Jesus is enough; I am broken; I cannot earn grace, but He makes me enough. That is what Jesus does.

We teach grace to our daughters like a slow drip coming from a runny faucet. We talk about it, offer undeserved favor, and model it. We talk about offering grace to siblings, friends and others in the community. We discuss that no one is perfect and practice praying for help when our daughters feel overwhelmed or insufficient. We teach them to turn to God and watch for the ways He shows up. We pray for God to fill in the cracks because He is enough.

In the throes of parenthood and life, it's easy to wake up each day with a sense of measuring our worth based on what we accomplished and the state of our children. We may measure their behaviors and development by how they are perceived by their teachers, Sunday school leaders, other parents, and of course our in-laws. Since the eve of social media and reality TV, like *American Idol* and *So You Think You Can Dance*, the next generations have become even more focused on becoming famous and "followed" in a way no one could have imagined fifteen years ago. It's remarkable how cultural norms have created a deep sensation to perform and wait for the "likes."

If Jesus lived in the 21st century, I doubt He would be on social media. That is not a judgment statement on whether or not we should be using social media, but rather an informed conclusion about who I have come to know Jesus to be and His heart for us. He is counter-cultural and yet so relevant to our basic common needs. He often said, "Do not tell anyone I am doing this," because He trusted the timing of others' discovery. We seem incapable of moving through our day until we tell everyone in our social media circles what we are doing. The younger we are, the more vulnerable we are to the web of messages in our societies. This may cause us to seriously pause and consider at what age our daughters should be allowed to use social media. This will be different for each family and for each daughter, but when we do let them, they need our regular coaching to help them discern how to use the platforms in healthy ways.

Coaching means we provide general guideposts to help our daughters navigate new and potentially damaging roads. The authors of *The Cure for Parents* say it this way: "A guideline is worthless to a one-year-old, but wonderfully life-giving to a ten-year-old. It gives more direction than directives. It employs a principle, a way of seeing, to help children understand how to navigate a variety of life decisions.

The guideline is relationally communicated, allowing children to own their choices in heartfelt obedience rather than compliance to a rule. It communicates consequences and the basis, protection, and freedom within the truth being given."[9] This is why the Courageous Girl curriculum is so powerful—because moms can have regular conversations throughout a daughter's young life that will strengthen her ability to navigate new choices ahead of her. Rules, or rigid theology, tell her what to do but never equip her for a time when the rules are not clear. We need to raise daughters who are able to think through their own choices before they act and can live with the consequences of what they choose. This intentional way of being helps Courageous Girls own their own decisions, discern potential danger, and lean into their relationship with God long after they are grown.

SHE KNOWS THE DIFFERENCE BETWEEN GRACE AND SHAME MESSAGES

Many of the issues we and our daughters struggle with are rooted in shame. The reason we seek approval from others is because God designed us with a longing to be seen, known and accepted. We have the privilege to help our daughters understand that only Jesus can quench this thirst. To learn this lesson, some girls will need to explore other waters so that they can compare the difference between true and false fulfillment. In any case, they get to choose whether they will receive grace or accept shame.

Brené Brown says, "I believe that guilt is adaptive and helpful—it's holding something we've done or failed to do up against our values and feeling psychological discomfort. I define shame as the intensely painful feeling or experience of believing that we are flawed and therefore unworthy of love and belonging—something we've experienced, done, or failed to do makes us unworthy of connection."[10] When we mess up or see our limitations in life, we can be in tune enough to experience conviction that compels us to change our behavior. We are loved and still mess up sometimes. One of the passages in scripture that is most dear to me gives voice to Paul, a former Pharisee who had to keep all the laws, who recounts how God uses his limitations and weaknesses to keep him connected to grace. He writes,

> Because of the extravagance of those revelations, and so I wouldn't get a big head, I was given the gift of a handicap to keep me in constant touch with my limitations. Satan's angel did his best to get me down; what he in fact did was push me to my knees. No danger then of walking around high and mighty! At first I didn't think of it as a gift, and begged God to remove it. Three times I did that, and then he told me,

> My grace is enough; it's all you need. My strength comes into its own in your weakness.

> Once I heard that, I was glad to let it happen. I quit focusing on the handicap and began appreciating the gift. It was a case of Christ's strength moving in on my weakness. Now I take limitations in stride, and with good cheer, these limitations that cut me down to size—abuse, accidents, opposition, bad breaks. I just let Christ take over! And so the weaker I get, the stronger I become. (2 Corinthians 12:7-10, The Message)

First, let me acknowledge that many have misunderstood or misconstrued Paul's words in this passage. I want to clarify that Paul's thorn is *not* an abusive relationship. Paul is talking about something in his humanity that limits him from what he would want to fully give to God. Though we do not know what this "thorn" was, and many have guessed, the weakness was not the point. Instead of wallowing in shame, Paul calls his limitation a "gift of a handicap." Staying in tune with our vulnerabilities and knowing we are loved are right in the pocket of grace.

The enemy wanted Paul to blame God. Paul could have said, "God hates me. I am not good enough. God is punishing me. I deserve better than this. I am unlovable." Instead, Paul knew God's heart and was attune to His voice. He heard the Father speak over him, "My grace is enough; It's all you need. My strength comes into its own in your weakness." The NIV says, "My grace is sufficient for you and my power is made perfect in your weakness." We have no need to hide our struggles, limitations or handicaps. As courageous mothers and daughters, we can be confident that His power fills in the cracks of our brokenness.

SHE SEES THE RAINBOWS OF HIS PROMISE

When I was in college in the late '90s, I was on a run to Gas Works Park in Seattle, Washington. Like most days, it was cloudy. On this particular day, the clouds seemed heavier and drearier, reflecting the weight of my soul. Even though it was probably misting, the raindrops felt like pellets on my face. I felt so alone and deeply troubled by the addictive behaviors of my eating disorder. I cried the whole way to the park and took my stance on a mound overlooking the water. My heart lamented, "I don't want this anymore!" As I looked up, the sky parted and the sun peeked its face through the clouds. Blue sky shone through directly over my mound. I felt the warmth on my cheeks as I wiped my tears. I looked around; it was raining everywhere I looked except right where I was standing. A rainbow soon appeared, and I was quickly reminded of God's promise to Noah. God spoke to me through the rainbow.

The sun quickly disappeared and though I jogged back to my dorm room in the pouring rain, my perspective had completely changed. God heard my cry and touched my soul. To this day, I can feel it in my body when I recall this memory. Through that experience, He showed me that the rain showers of our lives serve a purpose. While He will not always remove them, He will be present throughout them, giving us moments of warmth that sustain us through the storm. That day in Gas Works Park, I learned I was not alone. God showed me He is with me, painting a tangible truth in my spirit—the arc of my very own rainbow.

My daughters and I talk about rainbows regularly. We often remark how curious it is that rainbows require both rain and sunshine for such a beautiful phenomenon to occur. Such is life. The moments of amazing wonder, the grace that sustains us in hardship, the fact we are never alone—all these realities can keep our firm footing when the storm comes. A Courageous Girl can discern God's voice and live according to the grace and hope of His ways.

Takeaway

List as many of the lies you are tempted to believe about yourself, about others, and about God. Identify where that belief might have originated in your story. Ask God to show you if these voices are aligned with His truths and, if they are not, search for scripture to counter the voice that you are tempted to believe. Commit to memorizing one of the scriptures you find with your daughter and meditate on its truth for 90 days. See what God's power does in and through your weakness.

Take It a Step Further

Write out a timeline of your story. List out all the events in your life, good or bad, and identify what age you would have been during that event. Consider sharing your timeline with another person. See if you can discover any other shame-based beliefs life has taught you. Then bring all these events and beliefs to the foot of the cross.

5

She Knows Who She Is in Community

The person who loves their dream of community will destroy community, but the person who loves those around them will create community.

- DIETRICH BONHOEFFER, *LIFE TOGETHER: THE CLASSIC EXPLORATION OF FAITH IN COMMUNITY*

SHE JOURNEYS IN COMMUNITY

We have all felt alone at some point in our lives, sometimes in the midst of a crowd of people we call friends. Traveling the road of motherhood, especially in the earlier years, can be some of the longest, loneliest times. Throughout many years of private practice, I have listened to women share how hard it is to find friends they really trust. The void of authentic friendships in their lives leaves them uncertain and insecure about how to coach their daughters to foster relationships and manage other natural dilemmas that arise in female friendships. How do we handle mean girls? How do we prevent the formation of cliques? How do we find a best friend who will be faithful? What does a healthy friendship even look like?

No matter our place in life, we all have a need to be seen, valued, and to belong; it's knit into the very fabric of who we are. The desire to have a small tribe we call our own is common to all women. *No matter how introverted or independent we claim to be, we all long for a landing place where we can be ourselves.* As Christians, Jesus invites us into the deep waters of faith, and this often looks like intentional community.

One of those deep waters of faith is the space where relationships between women are created and nurtured. We all long for it, yet many of us only dip our toes in the shallow end. Women have a difficult time, to say the least, standing firm and being confident in female relationships. We approach relationships cautiously, hiding behind our masks and politely extending stiff arms to one another. The undercurrent of competitiveness and comparison cultivates insecurity, provoking women to bolt or triangulate rather than move toward one another. Our caution with female relationships can be exhausting, and just giving up is a tempting alternative. Ironically, clinical research shows that women generally desire closer emotional relationships than men. We have a great capacity to be known and know one another, and yet, at the depths of our souls, we fear this vulnerability. This fear causes us to sabotage relationships, sometimes even before they begin, with gossip, surface interactions, busyness, pleasing, avoidance, and more. If God created women with a deep desire for relational connection, why do we resist?

I have heard many women confess that they do not invest in female relationships to avoid "drama." I assure you, if you are raising a daughter you will be required to interact with other girls and their moms who regularly find themselves in the middle of this kind of relating. "Drama" does not have to be the end all. In fact, it can be a catalyst for change (good or bad) in each of us. Drama can be defined as "an exciting, emotional, or unexpected series of events or set of circumstances."[1] Most people love a good drama series on Netflix because they're packed with interesting characters and plot twists. Perhaps we can view living in community with others in a similar way.

When I read the Gospels, I find a lot of "drama." Personally, I could do without it, but when I remember that Jesus said all the laws depend on our love for God and others, I cannot deny that community is part of His plan. I want to help the next generation of girls, who are growing up in some of the most emotionally disconnected days in history, live like Jesus intended. This means they must be rooted in community. That begins with us finding or creating community wherever we go. Our girls will have an easier time embracing healthy community if we decide to go there first.

Whether we always seem to find ourselves in the middle of betrayal and hurtful relationships, or whether we've developed some clever coping strategies to protect ourselves from being hurt by others, we must face our fears and dive into the deep waters of community together. This is part of the reason why Courageous Girls groups ask moms to be involved *and* committed to one another over a long period of time. CG groups are not like other groups; we are deeply intentional, long-term communities of mothers and daughters who fearlessly address every issue that shapes the lives of girls today. Through years of practice, we aim to build healthy community before our daughters leave home. This group is one where moms and daughters go deep in relationship with one another, with female peers, and with God. Even dads will learn to have more meaningful relationships with their wives and other dads as they intentionally pursue their girls.

Humans are designed for intimacy—to be known and to know another. Trust is an essential ingredient for intimacy but can only be built with time, consistency, and, ironically, conflict. Most relationships do not arrive at conflict until two years into knowing one another.[2] This is around the point when the honeymoon stage ends. Many of us jump ship long before we get to see what God will do post-honeymoon and post-conflict. The journey of mothering girls is a journey of humility, one where we get the privilege (yes, privilege) of seeing ourselves in a new light as we participate in shrinking the gap between who we say we want to be and who we actually are, as well as between what we say we want for our daughters and what we actually teach them.

SHE GOES WHERE HER TRUST IS WITHOUT BORDERS

One of my all-time favorite worship songs is *Oceans*. I love the whole song, but there are six lines that God will not let me shake:

Spirit, lead me where my trust is without borders
Let me walk upon the waters
Wherever You would call me
Take me deeper than my feet could ever wander
And my faith will be made stronger
In the presence of my Savior[3]

My prayer is that He takes us Courageous Mamas to places where our trust is without borders.

Being known in community is necessarily one of these places because it requires intense vulnerability. Authentically participating in community requires us to trust God and others without reservation. It requires humility and the release of our clever coping strategies to hide. Trust draws us in to meet our deepest needs to be known and loved as we are.[4] So what keeps us from leaving the shore?

Acting courageously in a sea of women can be like swimming among blood-thirsty sharks in treacherous waters; most of us know this because we have been hurt by other females. I cannot tell you how many moms ask for help on how to help their own little girls navigate this "mean girl syndrome." If you wrestle with this issue, you are not alone. Courageous Girls groups are a response to those cries. As a fellow mom in the trenches, counseling, living out community and learning from moms that have gone before us, I am here to tell you that we can do this! Every generation has had some sort of "battle" before them. Eric Metaxas, historical and political author, says that though things look and feel really bad around us, the truth is that every generation, since the time of Christ, has thought it was the "end" of their time. However, God always raises up a remnant for His kingdom purposes.[5] The good news is that God is ever present and will raise up strong believers who stand firm in their faith to be a light in a dark world. Mamas, it is not by chance you are reading this book. We, alongside our daughters, can be those strong believers shining light to a dark world for such a time as this!

SHE'S NOT ALONE

Since the emergence of the digital age, while our "community" has broadened to global levels, our feelings of loneliness have increased. Technology is helpful for many reasons but has also contributed to the declining ability of girls (and boys) to meet their God-designed relational needs. The phenomenon worsens with each generation overly exposed to screen life. From the ways our brains develop to how we learn social cues, social platforms and digital devices create a negative return on societal investment. Their excessive use contributes to increased levels of bullying, depression, anxiety, insecurity and addiction. Researchers believe the digital invasion has become one of the greatest attacks on relationships and authentic community.[6] Relationship data says humans are created for fewer and committed friendships, reaffirming there is a point when we truly max out on the number of people we can manage in our lives.[7] In light of this ever-changing paradigm, our daughters need tangible examples of what it means to love, trust, serve, and move through life together with a few trusted individuals. Developing a Courageous Girls group is one way to put this truth into practice.

Choosing to join a group of moms and daughters for three to twelve years might sound intimidating, cultish, stifling, or exclusive. It's truly none of the above. Jesus models something profound with regards to community. He chose to invite twelve random men, who each had their own issues, to live in intentional community for three years. These men did not know Jesus was asking them to follow Him for three years exactly, but they knew Jesus was asking them for a commitment. This group of misfits were hand-picked and individually invited to follow Jesus. When they received their invitation, they hardly knew

Him. Even so, they said yes to His call. I believe they were longing for something more.

Jesus only had twelve disciples. He and those twelve ministered to thousands. Together, they wept, prayed, served, laughed, ate, walked side by side, and listened to one another. Among the twelve, Jesus even had a few with whom He was more intimate. According to the disciple John, he was the most "loved disciple." That's a pretty funny thought, isn't it? Jesus was closer to some than others, which gives His followers permission to be vulnerable with a few while loving and serving the many around us. This may come at a high cost. One of those close friends, Judas of Iscariot, betrayed Him. Anticipating this action, Jesus' response was to wash His betrayer's feet while he was still among the inner circle of friends. Jesus saw the war inside Judas and served him anyway: this is a reflection of the gift, complexity and cost of community living.

Given the costs of community, the temptation to hide and remain alone in life is completely understandable. Many Christians are afraid to be seen as exclusive, and that is the right heart posture. However, a fear of exclusivity can also become a rather clever way to avoid the risk of being fully known and loved by others. This was me. One of my best friends "confronted" me in the earlier years of our friendship with a statement that was hard to hear. She said that I had a gift to make everyone feel like they were my best friend, but it left my closest friends feeling insecure about their place in my life. It was cause for me to pause. Was making everyone my best friend what Jesus meant when He instructed us to love others like He loves us? Or was I just avoiding the chance of ever being betrayed by a Judas by cleverly staying safe in my friendliness?

Through prayer and intentional risk, I changed my approach to relationships. I asked female acquaintances to join me in my efforts to raise courageous girls. I trusted that if God was asking me to do this, He would orchestrate it. At the time I extended the invitation, the only commonalities I shared with the women I invited were an interest in Jesus and our daughters' attendance at the same school. I don't know if I was desperate or naive, but I like to believe that I was leaning into the Holy Spirit. Since that initial invitation, the moms and daughters in my group, along with their families, have become some of my family's dearest friends. They are our community. The bonus has been that our girls have had a chance to observe, learn, practice, and value the gift of "others" in our lives.

Originally, I was a bit shocked that these seven women said yes to my invitation; I was not even certain how I was going to lead us! But this has been the story of my life: go, and then God does something profound. For years, I had prayed for a group of gals to call my own; I knew that I needed a crew of women to help raise my girls in this harsh world. While my independent spirit made me feel like I did not want to be tied to such an intense responsibility, my clinical brain knew I needed to commit and press into these relationships, particularly the differences in our wirings, stories, and parenting philosophies. I knew conflicts would eventually arise (though I secretly prayed that we would be exempt from such hardships). On the other hand, my female brain was guarded; I had to fight the fear of letting these women in my life. Now I know we were all afraid, but each of us hosted anticipation and excitement as we banded together.

Because I have two daughters, I wanted each of them to benefit from their own Courageous Girls group. So, I led and hosted a Courageous Girls group for each of them. On the first mamas retreat, I invited both sets of women from each of the two Courageous Girls groups so that we had twelve women in total. At some point throughout the weekend, *every single woman* shared an insecurity with me. It was as though they were making sure I didn't change my mind about the invitation I had extended to them. If we feel this way as moms, we can be sure our girls wrestle with similar feelings.

Many confessed to ways they tried to wiggle out of the retreat just prior to coming. The specific voices in all our heads were different, but the common theme was *I do not belong.* There was the woman who looked put together but felt shame on the inside; the one who felt she was not pretty enough; the one who felt she did not know God or the

Bible well enough; the one who shared her childhood abuse and felt deeply afraid to be vulnerable again; the one who knew all the answers but felt alone and really unknown. I heard it all that weekend. I often wish I could bring all the women I have ever met—in and out of my office—just to say, "You are not alone in your insecurity." Even the well-known and beloved Beth Moore feels it. She really knows Jesus and the truth, and she wrote a whole book on this subject.[8]

One by one, I had quiet conversations in ordinary moments with these women. Together, we processed the feeling "I do not belong here." Time and time again, I found myself saying, "You belong here. We all are insecure—even me." (Heads would tilt in curiosity.) I expressed my own feelings to these women: "I have weaknesses I fear you all seeing, but I know in the core of my being that if we trust God, He will use this group to transform us into the women He designed us to be so that our daughters can follow us as we follow Jesus." No one else knew the others' insecurities, but as we all sat by a fire and laughed at "mama stories" that night, we shared our prayer requests. Slowly, we knew that God was doing something none of us could pinpoint. God was healing each of us with His slow and steadfast ways. He was showing us grace in the flesh. And He still is!

All women are inclined to fight that for which God created us: intimacy with Him and with one another. I tend to blame Eve for this. The Garden of Eden was a place where Adam and Eve had full access to be known by and belong to a safe and good God. When the enemy tempted Eve with a simple but crafty distortion of truth ("Did God really say, 'You must not eat from any tree in the garden?'"), you can hear his sarcasm and picture the smirk on his face. When Eve responded, the enemy continued to plant seeds of doubt in her mind. "You will not certainly die...For God knows that if you eat of it your eyes will be opened, and you will be like God, knowing good and evil" (Genesis 3:1-4, NIV). Today, the enemy continues to plant thoughts in our minds that God is not who He says He is. Eve had perfect intimacy in the palm of her hand, and she sabotaged it! Can you relate? It seems we question the intent of people's goodness. *They want something from me. It cannot be pure. There must be a hidden agenda.* Our insecurities rise.

From Eve's first conversation with the serpent, shame entered the Garden. It was in that place that we began to hide. The mask (or fig leaf in this case) serves as a false sense of protection or security. Adam and Eve found leaves and covered their "nakedness" so that they would not feel the shame of vulnerability. The need to hide ourselves is so powerful, but we fight it. Our girls fight it too. Prior to that moment, the Bible says they were "naked and felt no shame" (Genesis 2:25). Imagine what that would have been like! But after Eve ate the fruit, the battle of the sexes began: men started competing and women began scheming out of insecurity. The Genesis account says that when Eve saw the "tree of the knowledge of good and evil," she saw that it was "good for food, pleasing to the eye, and desirable for gaining wisdom." I will not go as far as to apply this to every woman, but I do think it's fascinating that Eve was tempted away from pure and true intimate relationship in the same way many of us use unhealthy coping strategies to find comfort in food, materialism, climbing the ladder or being knowledgable about subjects we love.

The American church and the modern lifestyles of our "global" world have fostered a false sense of community. Somehow, the church is buying into it. Even families are divided, busy, and rarely committed to one another. Yet we are designed for so much more. Because of who Jesus is, we can restore what was lost in the garden. Perfectly? No. However, by the power of the Holy Spirit in us, and through surrender to Him, we can have moments that resonate with original design.

We are meant to live a two-pronged approach: one is horizontal and the other is vertical. Similar to how the cross is designed, we are made for "horizontal relationships" with other human beings and a "vertical relationship" with an eternal God. Jesus is the center-point of it all. We are meant to discover love in both directions as we become more confident in God's love through our identity in Christ and as we grow more secure in loving relationships through the practice of community. Though different, the two approaches are not mutually exclusive. Instead, they are intertwined at the center of the cross.

SHE KNOWS AND IS KNOWN BY HER GOD

At the core of a woman who is confident, capable, compassionate and immersed in healthy community is a well-established identity. She knows who she is, and she knows how to connect well with others. She knows her identity is in what God thinks about her rather than how the world defines her. She knows what God says about her in His Word. Let's examine Psalm 139 and unravel the truths in this passage that counter the messages we hear in society today. Our God is so personal. Take a moment to meditate on this passage, pausing long enough to see which word, phrase or verse jumps out to you.

Psalm 139

1 You have searched me, Lord
And you know me,
2 You know when I sit and when I rise;
You perceive my thoughts from afar,
3 You discern my going out and my lying down;
You are familiar with all my ways.
4 Before a word is on my tongue
You, Lord, know it completely.
5 You hem me in behind and before,
And you lay your hand upon me.
6 Such knowledge is too wonderful for me,
Too lofty for me to attain.
7 Where can I go from your Spirit?
Where can I flee from your presence?
8 If I go up to the heavens, you are there.
If I make my bed in the depths, you are there.
9 If I rise on the ways of the dawn,
If I settle on the far side of the sea,
10 Even there your hand will guide me,

Your right hand will hold me fast.
11 If I say, "Surely, the darkness will hide me and
The light become night around me."
12 Even the darkness will not be dark to you;
The night will shine like the day,
For darkness is as light to you.
13 For you created my inmost being;
You knit me together in my mother's womb,
14 I praise you because I am fearfully and
Wonderfully made;
Your works are wonderful,
I know that full well.
15 My frame was not hidden from you
When I was made in the secret place.
When I was woven together in the depths of the earth
Your eyes saw my unformed body.
16 All the days ordained for me
Were written in your book
Before one of them came to be.
17 How precious to me are your thoughts, God!
How vast is the sum of them!
18 Were I to count them,
They would outnumber the grains of sand –
When I awake, I am still with you.
19 If only you, God, would slay the wicked!
Away from me, you who are bloodthirsty!
20 They speak of you with evil intent;
Your adversaries misuse your name.
21 Do I not hate those who hate you, Lord,
And abhor those who are in rebellion against you?
22 I have nothing but hatred for them;
I count them my enemies.
23 Search me, God, and know my heart.
Test me and know my anxious thoughts.
24 See if there is any offensive way in me,
And lead me in the way everlasting.

HE SEARCHES AND KNOWS ME

Psalm 139 is a powerful place to rest as a believer. As daughters of God, there is so much here for us to understand. Verse 1 says, "You search me and you know me." The intimacy of this statement blows me away, for all of us long to be pursued and deeply known. The image of someone "searching" me may sound invasive or irrelevant. However, every person, male or female, at some point in their life wanted to be known beyond Sunday morning small talk or polite work conversations. As a therapist, this is the gift I give to people: to be "searched" in a safe and non-invasive way that is respectful toward and in awe of a person's individuality.

Psalm 139 teaches that *because* He searches me, He knows me. The Hebrew word for "know" is *yada* and it has several meanings.[9] One is sharing love sexually, in the same way Adam and Eve *knew* each other to conceive their sons in Genesis 4:1,17,25. However, the other definition includes showing mercy and acting justly. We see this in other contexts throughout the Bible, such as Proverbs 12:10 and Jeremiah 22:15-16. The Lord knows you and me intimately—better than we know ourselves! God knows you in ways no one else can or will, and He continues to move toward us. He sees what others may be too busy to see. When no one else in the world seems to understand the depth of our thoughts and feelings, this is a powerful reminder. Even the closest person in our lives—our spouse, our parent, our best friend—does not know us like God does.

Psalm 139 continues that God perceives our thoughts and is familiar with all our ways. The word *familiar* points to the idea that you and I are not strangers to God, even if He seems like one to you. God is like a parent to a child. When our children were born, we knew the sound of their cries. I remember hearing a baby cry in the church nursery, and I could tell the cry belonged to my daughter. I knew her cry among the sounds of other babies. More than that, I was obsessed by figuring out the differences in my daughter's varying cries. Thanks to a random episode of *Oprah*, my husband and I could eventually discern the cries that signaled our baby's various needs: hungry, needing to be changed, tummy troubles or fatigue. We were so in tune and familiar with our daughter's ways, it became fun to meet her needs and see the relief in both our demeanors when we were able to do so. This is the kind of love God has for us! Becoming a mommy helped me to understand what it means to be *familiar* with someone.

We do not want to be women who know a lot about God and others while being disconnected from our heart and body. We must avoid being overly cerebral when we read the Word; it *has* to be digested if we want it to change every part of our being and doing. The Word is a love letter to us. And though God is the one who perfectly searches and knows us, He designed us in a way that we still need one another to embody this kind of care in the flesh. God's way of knowing us seems to be most tangible and experiential in the hug of another, a listening ear, a merciful response when we confess, or thoughtful gifts that point to details about us that only those who pay attention would catch. And yet, the hope that God intimately captures our hearts better than anyone else can bring us greater healing when our community is not there in the way we want or need. When we embrace the core truths of Psalm 139, we can risk more with other women because we always have a God who understands us when people disappoint.

SHE KNOWS AND IS KNOWN BY OTHERS

Many of our root issues in the counseling room stem from feeling alone. Being able to cope in a harsh world with lots of pain depends on the nature of our care team. The voices in our heads and hearts can steer us toward very destructive ways of living if left to ourselves. The independent mindset "I don't need others" breeds mothers and daughters whose days are based on whatever they feel, think, and experience. That's a risky posture to take and, from my perspective, counters everything I read in the Bible. We need to reconsider the plan God had for us originally, which is found in the powerful Greek word for community: *koinonia*.

In my late teens, I was sitting in a classroom with twenty eager young adults from around the country. Our professor gathered us around in a tight, awkward circle. With direct eye contact and precision in every word, he whispered, "You are Christ's body. All of you are the image of God in the flesh. Together, you are the body of Christ. You are the hands, the feet, the mouth, the ear, the heart… You are Christ to the world."

At that moment I began to understand the necessity of community, not only for our own sense of well-being but for the world to see the power of Christ here and now. I considered myself to be a loving person (you do too; admit it!), but at that moment I realized that the only way love can be reflected is through the dynamic relationships I have with others. Love (apart from God) does not exist in me alone. Love exists *between* you and me.

This powerful truth shaped the next steps of my life as I committed myself to learning to live in intentional community and helping others do the same. Community, though a cliché in many church circles these days, is a lost art in a culture that prides itself on being independent. Though we have swarms of "communities" gathered online and in the pews Sunday morning, living intentionally with others has become almost vintage, particularly on the West Coast. Maybe in your neck of the woods checking in on neighbors is still the norm, but most have become accustomed to living in silos under the assumptions everyone around us lives like we do. This is far from the truth. One advantage of my career as a therapist has been exposure to the vast variety of stories, cultures and meanings people live from, both consciously and subconsciously. I am better for it and have come to appreciate God's creative diversity in the body of Christ.

Recently, I was reading an article in TIME magazine about the gender revolution, a sensitive and very present issue today.[10] The article highlighted that we have moved from a binary culture, in which we once believed in two genders (male and female), to a culture that has two hundred different expressions of gender and sexuality. Whereas it was once culturally accepted that God determined gender, now each person determines their own sense of self. According to shifting cultural norms, we can now choose our child's gender or let them decide. God no longer decides. Raising girls in a world that has changed the entire definitions of gender identity has an impact on our daughters more than many can or want to imagine.

Within this new paradigm, "me, myself, and I" will determine who I am and who I will be, negating our entire need to help one another discover our sense of self. We have been told that finding ourselves is a venture we pursue all on our own—apart from our communities. This belief system reinforces the notion that we have the power to change ourselves based on our own feelings and desires. This ideology reestablishes the roots of what the Bible calls our sin nature and causes us to push God aside so that we can live the way we want. Though there seem to be many appealing aspects to the gender revolution, the social and neurosciences tell us something very different. We need each other to discover who we are, and leaving our identity formation to our own discoveries only perpetuates a downward spiral. At the outset, it appears that such "freedom to choose," even our own gender and sexuality, should bring peace. Rather, statistics tell us that we are more isolated, alone, and depressed than any generation before us. Could these be correlated at all? That might seem overly simplistic, but I beg to ask the question.

Not one of us reflects God without another. We need both genders, male and female, to reflect the image of God. In the third year of the CG curriculum, we dedicate a year to studying how to value our role and contributions within a greater community, as well as how to value others. We often trip over the arrogance that has been fanned by voices saying "you are enough" or "be who you are" without the caveat that we need community to reflect the fullness of God. The body of Christ, according to God's Word, is made up of male and female, as well as all nations, all tribes and the Gentile and Jew (see Galatians 3:28). Within that wonderful community lies a wide variety of personalities, gifts, talents, and experiences.

To be known, valued, invited, needed and honored is a remarkable witness to our independently minded culture. It's hard enough to live this out in our marriages; it's harder still to embrace this among those to whom we have made no promise or covenant. And yet the truth remains we are better together. Research proves this. Harvard did a longevity study on how relationships impact our overall health. The Harvard Gazette says, "Harvard study, almost 80 years old, has proved that embracing community helps us live longer, and be happier. Good genes are nice, but joy is better."[11] Our joy is made complete when we enter into community and allow the process to sanctify us.

SHE IS HEALED IN RELATIONSHIPS

If we have been wounded in relationships, one of the myths we tell ourselves is that *all we need is God*. Though this is true at its core, our greatest potential takes place in the center of human companionship. As humans, we have common needs to be loved, to dream, and to have purpose in the presence of others. Denying or vilifying these needs can wreak havoc on the soul and reveal false selves.

Doing life together can start in our homes and extend to others as we grow with fellow mamas and daughters. Remember what Henry Hendrix said: "We are wounded in relationships, but we are healed in relationships." And even more, we come to know who we are as individuals and our place of belonging within relationships. Ultimately, "finding ourselves" happens in the context of safe, grace-filled community where we are allowed to express a different opinion, share a doubt, or wrestle together with the greater issues in life. Sometimes this requires changing our community experience so that we are exposed to healthier environments. Sometimes this means we are the catalyst to help those around us move beyond surface commonalities to discover greater depths within a community in which God has already sovereignly placed us.

One of my former clients is a pastor and has fully admitted that if it were not for people, he would be a great guy. He struggles with loving people well and is honest about it. He loves theology, teaching the Word and administering all the details of the church, but the people...well, he could do without them. Loving them has been the hardest work in his ministry. He said all He needed was God, and He wished everyone else would get the same message. Similarly, a woman might join a women's group hoping to meet her best friend but never shares her struggles in the group. Consequently, she leaves frustrated, feeling that people did not take the time to get to know her. We all tend to place high expectations on one another, forgetting that God is the only one who can really love us perfectly. The reality of disappointment is a given, but it is not meant to keep us from pressing in. Dietrich Bonhoeffer said it this way: "Let him who cannot be alone beware of community... Let him who is not in community beware of being alone... Each by itself has profound perils and pitfalls. One who wants fellowship without solitude plunges into the void of words and feelings, and the one who seeks solitude without fellowship perishes in the abyss of vanity, self-infatuation and despair."[12]

No one is exempt from the fragility of human relationships. One of my greatest wounds was in the context of what I thought was a trusted relationship. After experiencing deep betrayal from an entire community, a dear pastor friend checked in on me and my husband. Our entire community had been blindsided by years of deceptions, and I told this pastor that I felt like I was covered in black tar. I did not know if I could enter back into community with others again after the ripple effect I experienced and watched unfold around me. At the end of our time together, he handed me a Costco-sized hand sanitizer to remind me that God would clean up the tar. He prayed that I would not harden my heart to others. I remember that prayer to this day, as the temptation to walk away from relationships with people in general was real.

Whether we expect too much or too little from people, what we find on the extreme end of the relationship spectrum is a desire to self-protect from the fragility of human relationships. We all have internal narratives that keep our walls up: *I need people; I don't need people; I am fine by myself; I should be fine by myself.* Both sides of the coin set us up for unnecessary pain. We were not designed with a need for isolation, nor with the desperation to find our worth in relationships, especially with those who continue to devalue and abuse us. The church at large has promoted the idea that God fulfills all our needs. *Yes, of course*

He does. However, He chooses to supply *some* of our needs through people.

SHE CHOOSES HER COMMUNITY WISELY

Choosing our inner circle can make or break the long-term health of a community; we need to make our choices wisely. Building relationships with people who can mutually strengthen one another consistently and over time is key. Trust cannot be built quickly, and anyone who claims differently should not be trusted! Brené Brown says, "Trust is a product of vulnerability that grows over time and requires work, attention, and full engagement. Trust isn't a grand gesture—it's a growing marble collection."[13] When we choose *who* we invest in, like Jesus did with His twelve disciples, we are free to live within our purposes. Choosing does not mean we are free from conflict, but it does mean we participate in it with the Holy Spirit. Christian psychologist Dr. Henry Cloud revolutionized Christians' understanding of healthy relationships when he co-authored the book *Boundaries*.[14] Cloud says, "Your relationship with God, your relationship with others, and your life practices are going to be the fuel of how you feel (about life and yourself), not what is going on around you." Those with whom we choose to spend our time impact our daughters far more than we know.

Girls today are bombarded with so many false witnesses of community; authentic community is hard to find. When invited to speak on relationships, my husband and I teach that the basic foundation of any healthy relationship is filtered through three questions: *Do I have a voice? Do you have a voice, Am I present?* One's "voice" represents our individual stories, wirings, needs, thoughts, feelings, and behaviors. Learning how to honor our own voice in any relationship starts with self-awareness. When our natural bent is to only focus on others, dismissing our own voice, *codependent* tendencies flourish. The church can often subconsciously encourage this kind of imbalance. On the other hand, if we are only aware of our own voice and disregard the voice of others, we travel quickly down the continuum of *narcissism.*

Creating space to honor both voices in any relationship is crucial to the sustainability of its health. Finally, being present means that we are not distracted by triggers from our past, worries for the future, or sensory overload by our current stressors. The gift of presence is no longer a given in our digitally charged world but rather a skill we have to learn and practice regularly with our daughters. When these three ingredients (my voice, your voice, and being present) are active in relationships, intimacy blossoms. If one ingredient is missing, the relational power is distorted. In this case, we see hints of dysfunction, such as control, manipulation, addiction, and protection, keeping us from experiencing deeper intimacy.

SHE KNOWS HER IDENTITY

Knowing our identity is one thing, but holding onto that truth when others see us differently is something else entirely. Healthy, grace-filled community directs us toward our God-given identity like a compass pointing toward true north. Being rooted in our identity in Christ means we discover what God thinks about us. Many of us never consider His perspective of us and sadly live in communities that forget to point us in that direction. God loves us. Becoming a follower of Christ is a very simple decision but is profound and life-altering. Knowing our identity in Him lays the foundation for a life of power and purpose. A Courageous Girl believes what God says about her. We need God-aligned, grace-filled communities to remind us of our identity.

I have found that there are thousands of women (and men) who profess Christianity and maybe even attend church regularly but never fully know what God thinks about them according to the Word. At the end of the day, there is no solid relationship with God the Father, Jesus the Son, and the powerful Holy Spirit. These women and girls may end up in our CG groups, or this might be you.

As I write about identity in Christ, I want to make sure the "entry door" to a relationship with God is unclear. Imagine a door that serves as the entryway to your life. God wants to be in your life, so He will knock at the door to see if He can enter. However, He will never violate our freedom and will, so He will wait at the door until we choose to open it. Some choose not to open the door, but even so He does not stop knocking and He does not leave. He is consistent in His pursuit of relationship with us. When we choose to open the door and invite Him in, He will walk through the door and will commit to be with us in every part of our life—good, bad, and ugly. In that intimate presence, He allows us to view ourselves through His perspective and plan for us and invites us to venture into a relationship with Him based solely on grace—unearned favor.

In light of not veering too far from the main point, I will share only one of the ways the Bible helps us know that Jesus is the way, the truth and the light. This concept for most today is very hard, because we do not want to leave any other faiths out of the picture. Can I just say that the invitation to have a relationship with God is open to everyone. In fact, *any*one, at *any* time, can come to God through what Jesus did on the cross and have a thriving relationship with Him. I do not know any other faith system that recognizes the depravity of man without requiring us to perform in order to be closer to God.

If you're new to the basics of Christianity, or to sharing those basics with others, I invite you to explore the "Roman road of salvation" concept found in the book of Romans (see 3:23; 5:8; 6:23; 10:9). The outline starts by explaining that we all fall short of the glory of God and can never measure up to His holiness. There is nothing we can do to restore our relationship with God on our own. I think we can all agree that humanity is far from perfect; even when we try to do good, our thoughts and our intentions can be twisted with selfish gain. Second, the penalty for the relational gap between God and humanity is death, but through Christ God offers eternal life. The Bible says Christ died while we were still sinners. This means that despite Eve's disobedience in the garden, through the death and resurrection of Christ, life itself is being redeemed. Finally, if you believe in your heart that Jesus died and rose for you personally, and if you declare with your mouth that He is Lord over your life, you are both "justified" and "saved."

Justification means we now do not have to earn our way to heaven, but instead we get to receive it! Salvation literally means God protects us from ourselves and the penalty due us. Both are grace. It can be hard for us to wrap our minds around free gifts; we always think there is a gimmick or ulterior motive. This is never the case with an all-good, all-loving God. He gives freely; all we need to do is open the door of our lives and receive all He has to offer us.

As child development research shows us, every child sees themselves through the lens of their parents. Whether we speak and treat our children with love or with contempt, annoyance and shame, the fruit of a parent's perspective and treatment of a child is reflected in the way that child carries themselves.[15] Christian parents are not exempt from this. We need an ultimate Parent who helps us see ourselves in the way we were created. When we become followers of Jesus, our identity transforms; we become who God says we are. When we accept God as our Father, He can parent us in a way that helps us assess how we see ourselves and reconstruct that image in the light. You are defined by your belonging: when you accept God the Father as your ultimate Parent, you affirm your belonging to His family and your identity as a saint. When you know who and whose you are, you know you have been made with purpose and equipped with courage to fulfill your God-given destiny.

Mamas, we are called to raise our daughters to know who and whose they are so that they can be courageous. It starts with our own relationship with God and how we link arms with others. Before you move on to the next chapter, take a moment to read a few of the verses from the Takeaway exercise and let them wash over your mind, heart, and body. This is not an exhaustive list, believe me. You may not believe these yet, but that is okay. Trust the process. Remember, discovering who we are takes practice in the confines of grace-based community where being known breathes life and meaning beyond our imagination.

Takeaway

Pick 3-5 Identity in Christ verses and choose to memorize them. You will find a list of scriptures in the back of the book .These verses will help you to discern who in your community helps you move toward truth. Identify a scripture that is hard to accept and ask God, and another person in your community, to help you grow in believing this truth. Give the list to your daughter and have her choose one or two scriptures she wants to memorize as well. Ask her which scripture is harder for her to believe and pray with her routinely about this struggle until you both recognize the difference in her spirit. As a challenge, attempt to memorize Psalm 139 with your daughter. Write it on a piece of paper and put it in a place where you will see it daily, like the bathroom mirror or the refrigerator. When we have God's Word embedded in our heart, we can steer our daughters, ourselves, and our community back to what He says about us.

Take It a Step Further

Does your community bring you back to your identity in Christ? Journal about a time when you felt safe, known, and seen in the context of relationships. Then write about a time when you felt unsafe. Take one practical step toward engaging in community and inviting people into your life. The first step is saying yes to the invitation from God.

6

She Makes and Keeps Friends

As human beings, our job in life is to help people realize how rare and valuable each one of us really is, that each of us has something that no one else has—or ever will have—something inside that is unique to all time. It's our job to encourage each other to discover that uniqueness and to provide ways of developing its expression.

- THE WORLD ACCORDING TO MR. ROGERS

It always helps to have people we love beside us when we have to do difficult things in life.

- THE WORLD ACCORDING TO MR. ROGERS

SHE INITIATES

Teaching a Courageous Girl how to be a good friend can be as difficult as teaching them how to fly. It's more complicated than we ever imagined and requires delicate training. As we interact with the different phases of our daughters' social lives, every wound in us regarding friendship seems to reopen. Wiring, circumstances, and coaching all play a role in how our daughters develop their sense of value, confidence, and safety within friendships. Some of us try to control them; others of us try to avoid them. Most of us are desperately praying about them.

I don't know about you, but I have always had to pray for friends. I remember moving many times as a girl; I would literally ask for a

Christian friend at each location. God provided every time, in every move, and in every situation. He did not always provide these female friends according to my timetable, but His provision never ceased to amaze me. So, if you want good friends for you and your daughter, first pray.

Second, if you want to have good friends, you need to be a good friend. If you wish others would extend an invitation, be the first to invite. Scottish pastor Alistair Begg once said, "The love of God is an initiative-taking love; in fact, genuine love always takes the initiative." Though this feels intimidating, and may trigger our fears of rejection and pride, this is the reality of where friendship begins. Someone needs to initiate. If you want to be friends with someone, I would challenge you to believe that God is asking you to take a step forward in faith.

Waiting for others to move can be agonizing and powerless. But inviting someone to coffee or organizing a playdate shifts the power. As adults, initiating invitations requires vulnerability; little girls start out having it a little easier. They begin with an innocent ideal that when you ask a friend to play, they will say yes. And if that friend says no, they simply play with another friend. Somewhere in elementary school, this changes. Girls start to acquire the same thinking as us adults, creating cliques to rule out who is "in" and who is "out." Being able to help our daughters navigate the world of friendship requires us to understand our own beliefs, biases and experiences about having friends. This is important so that we do not model out of our own wounds but out of what God has purposed for us all.

What we model in our adult friendships always speaks louder to our daughters than what we preach. Because of our unique wirings and our histories, we approach making friends differently. Having grace for our own hesitancies allows us to be patient with ourselves and our daughters. Alongside your daughter, learn how to be a good friend. Identify if you are a natural people person or prefer a more quiet day reading by yourself. Introverts, those who need more individual time, still need friends but prefer one-to-one or smaller groups. More extroverted people, those who like processing with others, enjoy meeting new people and having an extended network of friends. Think about your history of friendships and which relationships felt the most safe, healthy, and life-giving. Consider how those friendships developed and why they felt the most fruitful in your life. Ask why the friendship ended—because the seasons changed or because there was unresolved conflict? Then, begin to pray about who to start practicing with in your own community. Starting or joining a Courageous Girls group can be a natural step to practice developing healthier friendships for both you and your daughter. Finding trusting and lasting friendships requires action beyond what many of us want or are willing to do, but our daughters need to see the process in our lives if they're going to have sustainable friendships in theirs.

SHE REFUSES THE LIES WE TELL OURSELVES

As women, there are subtle lies we tell ourselves and sometimes even speak out loud that keep us paralyzed. These lies seep into the paradigms our daughters hold and keep up the walls that we are desperate to see fall. We might tell ourselves or others, "If she wanted to hang out with me, she would invite me to hang out." Or perhaps we might believe, "I am not valuable or worthy to be chosen as a friend." Maybe you have felt used in friendships and only called upon when needed for a resource or expertise. Maybe you have never had a friend whom you could trust with your deepest hurt. Maybe hanging out for the sake of relationships feels pointless or odd in some way. Many things keep us from moving toward one another.

As a girl who moved many times during childhood, I know what it is like to start over. When my family moved from Arizona to Washington state, I changed cultures, said goodbye to one of my best friends, and kissed the sun *adios*. The city of Puyallup welcomed me with ninety straight days of rain in a record-setting year. It was not an easy transition. Moving too many times as a child can be traumatic for many people. But in my case it built a skill set for which I have become thankful in my adult life. While there were many seasons of feeling unknown and trying to find some sense of belonging, being the new girl often meant I became popular quickly. However, that popularity did not translate to having deep friendships until I made a decision to pursue others.

I learned early on that, at some level, everyone is guarded and cautious to make a new friend. The way we perceive one another can be the greatest barrier. For example, I have a dear friend who is extremely introverted and gives off the impression that she is mad or arrogant. In reality, she is the most gentle and kind woman I know, but her face tells another story. Learning and teaching our girls the power of body language is a good place to start when teaching about friendship. Remembering to smile, making eye contact, and asking good questions are all simple ways we build connections with others. Finding the courage to initiate a conversation with someone we want to know better may be the only path to friendship with them. One of my life-long friends approached me on the first day of high school. Sporting her black high tops, she extended an invitation to her birthday party where I was brought into a group of girls I would have otherwise not known. I challenge you—be the first to extend the invitation. Yes, girls and women can be mean, but in many cases they are just insecure and cautious. If you initiate, you might find your best friend and a few other Courageous Mamas to journey alongside. If we can learn this lesson ourselves, we will be better prepared to coach our daughters when they find themselves in similar situations.

As I mentioned earlier, I barely knew any of the women I invited to join my first Courageous Girls group in 2012. Now these women have become my closest tribe of friends. I prayed for a group of women to travel with through motherhood and God answered. I am grateful they said yes to my crazy invitation. This was not easy for me, but many years of being the "new girl" gave me the courage to extend invitations to friendship as an adult. So many moms are waiting to be invited into community. If you have yet to find your tribe, start praying!

SHE HONORS HERSELF AND OTHERS

God has created a wide variety of people, and I happen to be someone who finds joy in that diversity. Learning what makes us unique helps us draw out others and honor their contributions in a relationship. Conflict often occurs because of misunderstandings, rather than true "sin" or intentional wrongdoings. God has created a variety of people to reflect the greatness of who we are and the depth of who He is.

My husband and I have used many personality assessments throughout our years in ministry, leadership development, and counseling. Our favorite has become the Core Values Index (CVI) created by Lynn E. Taylor, president of Taylor Protocols, Inc. in Seattle, Washington.[1] This instrument has an astounding 97% re-test reliability. This means that if you take this assessment every two years for the rest of your life, you will only find a 3% shift. Taylor's motivation for the tool comes from his bias that if you show someone who they really are then they will do something meaningful with their life.

The CVI explains a variety of ways we are motivated, communicate, learn, and handle conflict. Using the terms Merchant, Builder, Innovator, and Banker, the assessment reveals how much of each hard-wiring archetype we have within us. Knowing the amount of each Core Values God knitted in each of us explains our unique fingerprint. Though the assessment was not created with this in mind, we think all four Core Values reflect the image of God. Just like the four quadrants in the assessment, each person has parts of God's character to varying degrees. Our lack in one area points us to the fact that we need one another to be the Body of Christ. One is not better or greater than the other; instead, we complement one another.

In the assessment, each core value ranges from a low of 0 to a high of 36. The higher the number, the more intensely a Core Value is experienced in the outward expression of a person's life. Part of the genius of this instrument is learning what motivates, what creates anxiety and conflict, and how we can choose to shift from one Core Value to another based on what is needed in different environments and relationships. This becomes a powerful tool for mother-daughter relationships and for the development of healthy Courageous Girls' groups. Here is a very brief overview of each Core Value, which is explored purposely throughout the CG years.

Merchants are highly relational individuals who live out of truth and love. For merchants, truth is the ability to see things the way they are and love is the ability to honor the core values in one's self and in others. Merchants are visionaries and love to encourage those around them. They think about how their relationships are affected as they move through life. Merchants love to communicate and feel their way through the world. They have X-ray vision for people's emotions. They learn and communicate through verbal processing with another human beings. Without the merchant, we would miss the need to connect and celebrate. Merchants love nothing better than a party to celebrate others or a reason to cast vision beyond what others can see possible.

Builders are task-oriented people who live out of power and faith. Their power is used to make a positive difference and their faith is the ability to know what to do. They do not want or need to read the instruction manual when trying something new. They have an intense need to close the deal, finish a task, and love to encourage others to do the same. They are the action and results-oriented members of the community; they learn by doing. They communicate with a few intentional words. Without the builders, the rest of us would talk or think our way through life without ever acting upon our words and ideas.

Innovators are systems thinkers who live out of wisdom and compassion. Their wisdom is both the ability to see the way things are and to know what to do about it, and their compassion is the capacity to remain inquisitive until all the data is collected. These are the wise sages of the group who can often think outside the box and hold messy, complex problems well. They can be taken advantage of because they are the problem solvers in the community. They may find themselves having a hard time saying no due to their steadfast compassion. They learn by assessing solutions in their mind and communicate complex thoughts. Without them, the community might do the same thing over and over again without getting new results. Like their name, this group finds joy in innovating and creating new solutions for the community.

Bankers are fact-driven people who live out of knowledge and justice. They love to be organized, precise, and gather the facts.

Meet at twelve o'clock in the afternoon means arrive sharply at noon. They tend not to speak unless they are certain of what they are sharing. They are thoughtful, as they remember details about others in ways the rest of the community misses. These people care about equity in the community and will notice when others are missing resources or are being treated unfairly. They learn by reading information and communicate with others by giving detailed, linear data after being sure of what they have to say. Without the banker's "black and white" meter detecting right from wrong, we would miss out on order, precision, and justice.

When we can notice others and the way they bring value to our community, something profound occurs: Kingdom living. So often we are tempted to raise our daughters to be like us as moms, but seeing a daughter's unique wiring can help us know how to partner well with her and assess where conflicts might arise, as well as help her build confidence around her own God-given contributions to the world. This is where knowledge can equip us in ways to fan the flame of our daughter's gifts and prevent us from overshadowing her sense of self. This can give us great direction on how to parent as well as show grace.

For example, my oldest and I are different in a few key core values. We talk about this openly and have found ways to navigate her frustrations with my lack of attention to detail. Similarly, I have grown in ways that encourage her ability to cue into the details. Rather than moving into the "you do not understand me" phase, she knows that I am trying to honor her "Banker" value by giving her the ability to research our family vacations, organize CG gatherings, and share the many facts she learns as she reads and absorbs information at school. My hope is that all of our girls will not only leave our homes feeling ready and equipped to be who God made them, but they will be so self-confident they won't compare themselves to siblings or other girls. Rather, they will see one another as a partner, not as competition, in the greater work God is doing. We need every single core values—the idea person, the people person, the task person, and the detail person—to reflect the glory of God.

The comparison game comes from a place of insecurity—not knowing who we are and wanting to be like someone else. It's a normal but deadly trap that sucks energy never intended to be spent in such a way. In fact, the CVI tells us that when we are trying to live out of the core values in which we score lower, we are not only causing greater angst in our emotional and mental health but also cutting the world short of our greatest contribution to the wider community. God did not design us to drift slowly from our hard wiring and God-given design. Instead, we are to embrace the strengths and the limitations as a way to give and receive in community. Friendships are a way to partner together to face life's hardships, like illness, job losses, death, family difficulties. And yes, even when our children are struggling, friendships are meant to provide the support, prayer, and encouragement we need to walk them through their own difficult moments.

Often friendships are formed, but fade fast over small misunderstandings or differences. Many times these differences are simply related to how people are wired; different wirings have different communication styles. Sometimes, we are (figuratively) speaking a different language and do not even know it. If we learn to name the ways we are similar and different, we will begin to honor ourselves and others. In this process, we will transform our approach to building relationships and communicating with others and will create longevity in our friendships.

SHE IS COMMITTED THROUGH THE CONFLICTS

The Bible is very clear that finding a friend is like finding a ruby. So keeping a good friend is worth it! Proverbs 20:6 says, "Many will say they are loyal friends, but who can find one who is truly reliable?" It may not seem encouraging at first, but I find this verse helpful because it validates the difficulty of finding and keeping good friends. It might be easy for some to make friends, but it takes great character and integrity to keep them. If you are friends with anyone long enough, and if you are really going deep in your relationship, conflict is bound to happen. If you do not experience any conflict, then your relationship is still treading water and has not ventured into the deep end of the pool yet. A long time ago, I decided that in order to teach my girls how to be friends and keep friends, I would have to learn to do the same in my life. That means moving through conflict rather than around it. The natural people-pleaser in me would rather smile and stuff my own feelings of hurt, but I have been a therapist long enough to know that is not a viable way forward.

Dealing with conflict can feel like extra work and unwanted drama for many of us. However, our unhealthy coping patterns can take more effort than healthy ones. In fact, if we dig further into the CVI, we learn that each wiring has its own style of conflict, each of which is poisonous to healthy relationships: the Merchant will manipulate; the Builder will intimidate; the Innovator will interrogate; and the Banker will become aloof in judgment. (This is covered in Year 5 of the CG curriculum.) These conflict strategies arise whenever we feel like our Core Values are not honored by another. These responses to conflict look different depending on a person's unique wiring. However, in all cases, the energy it takes to live out of our conflict strategies, rather than trying to approach conflict in a healthy manner, moves us away into isolation and further from meeting our truest needs of restoration and intimacy.

It takes energy to ignore someone, employ passive aggression, withdraw our love, blow up in anger, gossip, build alliances, defend our case, or pretend like everything is okay. The anger, guilt, and resentment we carry under the surface can be just as destructive as saying the wrong thing or being rejected. Conflict isn't always negative or unproductive; in fact, many research studies have shown that quantity of conflict in a relationship is not as important as how the conflict is handled. When conflict is managed well, it has the potential to lead to more satisfactory relationships.[2] Even God would rather us come to Him with our doubts, hurts, concerns and fears, and wrestle honestly with Him, than remain distant for the sake of "keeping the peace."

Conflict is a necessary ingredient in the process of being known and building intimacy. Without it, relationships remain shallow, and one will never know if they can be trusted in a storm. The very essence of our faith is rooted in a narrative that moves through conflict. Drs. John and Julie Gottman, marriage experts in the clinical world, run a relationship lab in Seattle, Washington, where they literally watch couples experience life together over long periods of time. After almost forty years, they have consistently found that the number-one predicting factor in whether or not a relationship will last is how they handle conflict. They say that they can predict the longevity of a relationship at 97 percent accuracy![3] Since our children learn these skills in the home they grow up in, moms (and dads) are the key teachers in this area.

The next logical connection is that in order to mother a Courageous Girl well, we must learn how to fight fairly ourselves. Conflict only becomes toxic when it is ignored and unresolved. It begins to ferment in our souls and create side effects. There is a direct correlation between the health of a relationship and how quickly that relationship repairs their hurts. This means that once you have wounded one another, which happens in every single human relationship sustained over time, the length of time it takes to work through the hurt directly reflects its health and sustainability. Fighting fairly means that we play by the "rules" and leave out what the Gottmans call the "Four Horsemen of the Apocalypse"—criticism, defensiveness, contempt, and stone-walling. Instead, we should use healthy communication so that both parties can be heard and understood, taking any actions needed to make amends so that we can draw closer to God and one another.

These principles are powerful ones, *and* they align perfectly with God's Word. This is my favorite part of research! It continues to improve each year, proving the wisdom of God and the practicality of the Bible. The Gottmans say that "repair," the attempt to get a relationship back on track, is the secret weapon of emotionally connected people. They say that repair is "any statement or action—silly or otherwise— that prevents negativity from escalating out of control." Every other relationship expert, including the Lord, would agree that the heart behind trying to move toward someone rather than away from them is a healthier starting point.

One of my favorite parts of the Christian faith is that we are not asked to be perfect and that we have a remedy for when we mess up—the help of the Holy Spirit. Though some believe that the context of Matthew 5:48, "Be perfect, therefore as your Father in heaven is perfect" (NIV), literally means that Christians should have no sign of sin, this kind of thinking keeps us from maturing in our faith journey and leaning into the transformational power of Christ. Simply, it alludes to the idea that if you are not perfect, then you are not a follower of Jesus. In reality, the more mature we are in our faith journey, the more aware we are of our sin nature. We are slower to react to others and therefore press deeper into the strength of the Holy Spirit and the wisdom of the Word. The more we mature in our faith journeys, the quicker we become in recognizing our own limitations and accepting the power of God through our human weaknesses.[4] As Trueface Ministries puts it, we come out of hiding and begin to face the reality of our condition with God and others.[5] This is a life-long process, knowing that we will be made complete when we see Jesus face to face in heaven. I pray our Courageous Girls capture this message of grace because it's the lens in which we maneuver through our friendships. This way of thinking helps us see a key difference between being human and sinning, though both can create conflict. When they do, both require moving through *repair* with those around us.

Some years ago, on a leisurely Saturday afternoon, I decided to go shopping with my daughters. The three of us joyfully jumped in the car, and I, as usual, drove my car out of our garage, maneuvering in my typical manner to ascend up our gravel driveway toward the road. As I turned to leave our country home, I heard a *bang!* To my utter surprise, I hit our friend's parked car *right outside my home*. I was in a car accident in my own front yard! No one was hurt, but my girls watched me lean my head into the steering wheel to pray out loud. (I did not start singing Carrie Underwood, but I sure felt the need to have Jesus take the wheel.)

Before I could get out of the car, my husband, Jeff, and our dear friend (the car's owner) came to check on us. I could see by Jeff's face that he was trying to make a split-second decision: either to be mad at me for such a clumsy move or to have compassion for me as he saw my embarrassment and remorse. If I had looked in my rearview mirror before exiting the garage, I could have avoided the situation. But no… not this time.

As my daughters watched the drama unfold, they learned many lessons. Instead of being met with anger, I was met with comfort and concern. Our friend's car was quite damaged in the collision outside my driveway, and Jeff and I both assured him we would make it right on our end. After a brief assessment, we all went on our own ways: the girls and I went shopping, and the men continued to hang out. Immediately, insecurity set in. I thought of my friend and his wife, both Bankers in the CVI index: careful and thoughtful people with a potential for aloof judgment. My core values began to emerge: the Merchant inside me wanted to cry; my Innovator wanted to blame the situation on our friend for choosing to park where he did. (Even though he used the same spot everyone uses when they visit our home!) Wanting to feel the shame of my careless move, an internal voice communicated that no one else had ever done something like this in their driveway. Then panic set in as I considered that my mistake could cause my friends to judge me, mistrust me, and possibly keep their distance from me.

Before my daughters and I had reached our destination, my husband and our friend's wife (one of my CG mamas) left me separate voicemail messages that I played out loud to my girls. Careful and thoughtful, each of them wanted to communicate they understood that what I had done was simply a mistake. They added that they were praying the mishap would not ruin what my daughters and I had set out to do that afternoon. Their concern was moving, and I shared with the girls that both people could have responded very differently to my actions. However, in their grace for me, I was set free to be fully present with my daughters. I texted Jeff back, saying, "Because my identity in Christ is rooted in what God thinks of me, I am free to own this mistake and make it right. I own every part of hitting our friend's car and am grateful for the grace he showed me. This is a sober reminder that the ever clumsy and fast-moving Terra still remains after forty years trying to slow down!—in every sense of the words. Thank God for these reminders and to know I am loved in the midst of something that could cause guilt, shame, and a ripple effect of other poor behaviors."

I have taught conflict-resolution skills for years to every kind of person. It seems that those whose identity is rooted in Christ have an easier time moving through the heat. Being rooted simply means that I know who I am because of what God says about me and that my circumstances, choices, or others' opinions do not dictate my value or worth. After my accident, I could have held the guilt of hitting our friend's car for days, months, years. However, Christ says I am loved, forgiven, redeemed, and a work in process that He will finish. Knowing these identity statements frees me up to be human and know what to do when I mess up. Remember what Dr. Landreth says: "It's not always what you do, but what you do *after* what you did that matters most."[6]

Because I know I am loved, I can: (1) own my choices and mistakes; (2) recognize the consequences I caused to the other; (3) empathize with their pain; (4) ask for forgiveness; and (5) make it right, if I can. In my situation, "making it right" meant starting an insurance claim on our end and confirming that our friend's car was cared for as soon as possible. I could not go back in time, but I could make sure I learned from my mistake. (In case you were wondering, I drive very slowly out of my garage now.)

If I find my identity only in what I do, then moving beyond my mistakes can turn into lingering shame, defensiveness, blame, minimizing damage, denial, and more. For some, even the act of making things right leaves a lingering guilt and a desire to hide. We need to remember that this kind of "conflict" happens all the time, and if we react poorly it can lead to bondage and relationship ruin. If we learn to handle conflict well, our children will benefit from our mistakes. I saw the car accident as a teaching moment, and I tried to help my daughters process what they saw and noticed at the first opportunity.

I even overtly explained how Daddy and I would make it right and admitted out loud, "What happened was my fault." I pointed out the difference between how our friend could have responded and how he actually responded. I pointed out that I was given grace, patience and gentleness, and that I was grateful for it. The conversation was better than I could have expected, and I appreciated the chance to impart a real-life lesson.

The word "conflict" means "to come into collision or disagreement; be contradictory, at variance, or in opposition; clash."[7] Despite a few personalities who delight in debating, most people prefer harmony and would rather dismiss their own voice for the sake of keeping peace. In fact, many Christian cultures teach this kind of thinking: it is better to have peace than to make your own voice heard. I believe this concept confuses the idea of humility with codependency and passivity.

Humility, in its purest definition, is having a sober mindset of ourselves. We are neither better nor worse than any other. Philippians 2 tells us that Jesus modeled humility as He left His throne of glory and humbled Himself to become a baby boy, entering our world and choosing to restrain His power. Jesus was not less than us. Instead, His humility was in His choice to submit, out of love, to God the Father and to join us in our human existence. I have come to understand submission as a love word rather than a powerless word. As females in the church, we are cultured to be sweet and quiet. Even beyond church culture, an outspoken woman can be perceived as a witch. (Feel free to switch out the "w" with another letter...you get the point.) However, Jesus' model of humility is for both males and females. Jesus did not take a passive role but rather an assertive "on mission" role that makes choices out of love, purpose, and grace.

When you know who you are, you do not need to convince others of who you are; this is humility. If we become comfortable with who we are, we will speak truth to one another. Our mere backgrounds, wirings, and broken humanity will create moments of potential collision. Proverbs 27:5-6,17 says it beautifully: "Better is open rebuke, than hidden love. Wounds from a friend can be trusted, but an enemy multiplies kisses...As iron sharpens iron, so one person sharpens another." A faithful friend will move through conflict with you and will not offer you fake kisses or hidden love. She will speak to you with truth and trust you with her heart. She will tell you when she was offended and needs repair. She will own her mistakes and, instead of defending them, she will try to make them right. She will empathize with your perspective and learn how to serve you even if it's different than her ways. She will not avoid you, but she will pray and trust that God will show her how to make amends. Courageous is the woman who is committed through conflict and humble enough to honor her own needs alongside the needs of others.

SHE HAS BOUNDARIES: RED LIGHT, YELLOW LIGHT, GREEN LIGHT

Many are confused by how to move through conflict, especially when it's time to set a boundary with a hurtful person who has "sinned" again us repeatedly. Confusing messages, often meant with good intentions, have left many women and girls uncertain of how to discern when it's time to close a door on a friendship or continue trying for repair. Not all friends will remain close friends, even safe friends, and the Bible is clear about this. Matthew 18 is wholly dedicated to addressing someone who continues to wrong us and is unwilling to own their mistakes or turn away from their hurtful ways. Through time and tested conflicts, we learn whether a friend is a red, yellow, or green-light friend. The CG curriculum helps to process this issue in various ways at each age level since it is such a vital part of being a Courageous Girl. Using the analogy of a traffic light that gives clear direction to vehicles on the road, there are three types of relationships we need to consider as moms raising daughters.

Red-light people are those who do not respect our boundaries and, even when we have asked for change, dismiss our voice, continuing on as if their needs are the only ones that matter. These red-light people are considered unsafe; it would be enabling to maintain a relationship with them or ask our daughters to do the same. Red-light people are those who do harm to others and have no remorse or changed behaviors. They may even say they are sorry but their actions will reveal whether or not they are truly repentant. Repentance literally means to make a 180-degree turn and move in the opposite direction. Those whose words cannot be trusted, and continue harming people, can be what the Bible calls "wolves in sheep's clothing": they delight in doing wrong and are unwilling to change. The color red, like in a traffic light, symbolizes the need to stop the relationship altogether until there is evidence of full repentance over an extended period of time (two-plus years is a safe reference point in these cases). Red-light people will not understand and will likely make you out to be the "bad guy." Boundaries in these cases will need to remain very high. The application of this principle must be used wisely, prayerfully, and with great counsel.

Yellow-light people are hot and cold. Some days they respond to your needs, other days they talk about you behind your back. They might not harm you or others on purpose, but they are what the Bible calls "fools" because they blame the circumstances around them rather than owning their own participation in the problem. These friends are repentant at times and may not overtly try to hurt us, but they are inconsistent and cannot be fully trusted. Similar to a yellow light in traffic, we slow down and are cautious with these friends. We are kind, respectful, and often associate with these people still. However, we do not let these people into our trusted inner circle unless they show healthy movement toward becoming a green-light person.

Green-light people are friends who make mistakes and have bad days, but they are always willing to own their behaviors and make things right. Their intent is never to harm you. These friends may go through hard seasons and may not always be the best of friend, but that is when you get to serve them and be the friend they need. The tides will change and one day you will have your turn. Green-light friends are trustworthy; they speak truth, work through the conflicts, and move toward forgiveness. We can see repentance in their changed behaviors and they follow through on what they say. The Bible calls these people "wise." They are not perfect, but they demonstrate a heart that wants to remain in a right relationship with you and God.[8]

SHE CONFESSES AND FORGIVES

Ruth Haley Barton once said, "One thing we can know for sure is that when we are confessing our sin to God but not to the people around us in ordinary, nitty-gritty life, there is not much real spiritual transformation going on."[9] When we are in courage and surrounded by a community of moms who allow us to be ourselves authentically, then we can confess to one another the hidden places of our hearts and souls. Confession is not always the expression of something we did wrong but can be the confession of all of who we are: our dreams, hopes and shortcomings. Have you told anyone your childhood story? Have you ever shared your greatest fears or the shame voices you hear in your head? James 5:16 says, "Therefore confess your sins to each other and pray for each other so that you may be healed. The prayer of a righteous person is powerful and effective." Transformation and healing can occur when we open our mouths and tell one another what is really going on inside of us. Friends who are willing not only to listen but to safely acknowledge our struggle and pray for us, rather than judge or try to fix us, are the kind that bring healing. Some of the latest research has shown us that our brains are literally repairing as we empathize with one another.[10] I wonder if that is why God asks us to confess to one another.

To tell another human being what we can own in our own lives is just as courageous as forgiving someone who has wronged us. Forgiveness is more profound than most of us realize. It is not the absence of caring, nor is it merely brushing things off. In fact, it is quite the opposite. We often say trite things like "forgive and forget" or "forgive as God has forgiven you." However, these phrases do not fully embrace the extended facets of forgiveness. God does not forget; He chooses not to remember. That is the difference between a willful choice and a momentary absence of mind.

The Hebrew word used for "forgive" is *nasa'*, meaning to lift off, to carry away or literally to let go.[11] In order to forgive, we need to know what we are letting go. A simple way to forgive that both honors the heart and the profound nature of what forgiveness is meant to be follows these steps. First, name the offense, recognizing its consequences and how it made you feel. Then, grieve. Depending on the offense, the grief will have different lengths of time. Then, choose to let the offense go into the hands of a just God. Many of us need to be reminded of the ways God is just in order to hand over the pain of others' known or unknown harm against us. We need to truly wrestle with and hold tight to how our righteous God is both merciful *and* faithful to meet the evils of this world with a right response. As we read through scripture, we find that His justice is not always aligned with our idea of it, but He is surely a God who sees and will make all things right someday. This process is not the only way to forgive, but for me it has become the way that feels the most concrete and transformative in my life and others'. It is important to note that the choice to forgive is truly one of the last steps in any healing process, though Christians often suggest it is the first.

Jesus journeyed through the Garden of Gethsemane, feeling the weight of His choice to forgive, before He gave His life on the cross. Working with survivors of sexual abuse and sexual betrayal, the notion of forgiving before grieving not only feels like re-traumatizing a survivor but also seems entirely unbalanced. Choosing to forgive often requires a clear sense of boundaries and a healthy restoration of a person's power to choose. *Mending the Soul* by Steve and Celestia Tracey, a beautifully crafted biblical and trauma-informed recovery book and workbook, helps unravel the complexity of forgiveness and why it is okay to take time to forgive as well as refrain from restoring relationships with unrepentant red-light people.[12]

Courageous girls understand that forgiveness is not just a word we flippantly throw around but a transformational process that helps us stay aligned with God and others. The steps of moving through forgiveness allow our full person to move forward: soul, brain, mind, heart and body. We help our daughters disrupt cycles of abuse and value their own worth as women. Telling a daughter to "forgive" an abusive person[12] before protection occurs only puts her in the way of continued harm. Through the process of naming and feeling the emotions associated with the offense, and then choosing not to punish someone for what they have done, allows God to do as He sees fit. He will offer the abuser either mercy or justice, but the point is that it's His decision. Forgiveness does not equal trust or relationship restoration. We can forgive *and* keep our boundaries in place with those who are unrepentant and unsafe. This brings a small amount of comfort in the face of all the awful abuse humanity has experienced.

Most of the time, we are not forgiving abusive dynamics but rather miscommunications and clumsy collisions. There are times when this forgiveness process must take place between me and God. I take this opportunity to pray the forgiveness process out loud or write it in my journal as a letter to Him. I can do this even when I do not have relationship with a person any longer. In healthier relationships, I can take the grievance directly to my friend. Matthew 18:5 says that if your brother or sister has sinned, go and point out their offense. Matthew 5:23-24 says that if you remember that your brother or sister has something against you, go to them before you bring your gift to the altar. In either case, you are to go to the person and confront them, not wait until they magically recall they offended you. Expecting someone to know they hurt you or offended you is not a realistic expectation. This is called *mind-reading,* and I am not sure I have met anyone who does it well. Often, we do not know we have hurt someone else until we are told. But if our relationship is a green one, then we will work through the conflict with confession and forgiveness until we are right with one another again.

I will leave you with a few final reminders that help us moms navigate our relationships in ways that teach our daughters to as well. Forgiveness is not equated with trust. Trust is built over time and consistent actions with repentant hearts. In order for a relationship to reconcile, forgiveness must happen. However, forgiveness can happen without reconciliation. Reconciliation requires two parties who are willing to own and change behaviors in order to rebuild trust. Recalling the hurt from our relationships with others can be a reminder of how God has faithfully rescued you and given you wisdom and discernment for present relationships. Forgiveness is a process that recognizes the gravity of harm done and, in doing so, helps us honor our own emotions, mindset, and experiences for deeper healing and lasting change.

Working through conflict and learning to forgive are the final ingredients of a healthy, quality friendship. No true friend is made overnight; friendship takes slow and steady investment, intention, and conflict management. Making friends can be the first hurdle, but keeping them is where Courageous Girls find the depths of God's heart for His church. This is where we all grow as children of God and experience intimacy as we become vulnerable, real, and honest with each other. A girl who has one to three friends who will go the distance with her is truly rich. As the Word says, who is really faithful? A Courageous Mama and her daughter can be faithful because of who Jesus is and what He does in and through us as we allow Him to lead the way.

Takeaway

Make a list of the women in your life. See if you can discern prayerfully who is a red-, yellow-, and green-light friend. If you need to set some boundaries with your red- and yellow-light friends, write down one or two boundaries you will put into action this week. Tell your green-light friends how grateful you are to have them in your life. Write them a card or send them a text to remind them of their role in your life. If boundaries are hard for you, consider reading the book *Boundaries* by Dr. Townsend and Dr. Cloud. If you do not have any good friends you can name, prayerfully ask God to bring them into your life. If God brings anyone to mind, initiate a coffee date!

Take It a Step Further

If you need to work through unforgiveness, start by writing down the names of people who have hurt you and what behaviors they have done. Write down how each offense has made you feel and list any consequences that have occurred since the offense took place. Ask the Lord if you are to go and talk to your friend or work through your forgiveness with Him. In either case, identify if this hurt results from a personality conflict or a sinful behavior. Finally, consider any part you have contributed to the hurt. You may be completely innocent, but Matthew 18 reminds us that before we are to go to a brother or sister about how they have wronged us, we need to make sure we have assessed our own hearts and can approach them with gentleness.

Second, practice asking your daughter for forgiveness any time she tells you about a hurt you caused her. If she tells you that you have hurt her, that is a huge step forward for your relationship! It means you are safe for her to be honest. Practice saying the words "Will you forgive me?" Invite her to participate in the forgiveness process by offering you the words "Yes, I choose to forgive you" or "I need some time, Mom." Both responses are okay. Each wiring needs different things for closure. The Merchant needs to see emotional remorse. The Builder needs direct ownership with no excuses. The Banker needs time and wants to see you make it right. The Innovator needs to understand the context and reasons behind the behavior. Remember to tell your daughter how you will intentionally make it right. This pattern will help you both learn how to practice forgiveness outside of your relationship with friends in and outside of your CG group.

7

She Is Fearless...Almost

Being brave isn't the absence of fear. Being brave is having that fear but finding a way through it.

—BEAR GRYLLS

I have learned over the years that when one's mind is made up, this diminishes fear; knowing what must be done does away with fear.

—ROSA PARKS

SHE FEEDS HER FAITH, NOT HER FEARS

When I think about what I want for our daughters, I think of freedom from fear. By fear, I mean the kind that causes us to live limited lives. Fear of doing what God is asking of us. Fear of being ourselves. Fear of ruining our daughters. Fear of messing up. Fear of success. Fear of the world, and so forth. God longs to help us and our girls move through these kinds of fears, asking us to replace it with something far more powerful: faith.

There is a pillow in my living room that reads, "Let your faith be bigger than your fears." I am always reminded of Queen Esther, an ordinary woman with wounds of her own who was used for extraordinary circumstances. Esther was a beautiful young virgin in the land of Persia. Even though she was orphaned and cared for by her older cousin Mordecai, she was chosen to be queen through a very vain beauty pageant. Mordecai counseled her not to reveal her Jewish heritage as she took the throne. God used Esther's beauty and poise to win the king's favor and positioned her in a pivotal point in history. God used all of who she was, even her looks, for the greater good.

This king was easily persuaded, and he had agreed to kill all the Jewish people throughout his kingdom. Esther could not stand for this atrocity and decided to make a request to spare their lives. Just before Esther approached the king to ask him to save the Jews, she said to her cousin, "Go and gather together all the Jews of Susa and fast for me. Do not eat or drink for three days, night or day. My maids and I will do the same. And then, though it is against the law, I will go in to see the king. If I must die, I must die" (Esther 4:16, NLT).

If I die, I die has become the theme of my life (sometimes with a little nervous giggle under my breath), as I have tried to face my own fears and build the muscle of courage in a world where it seems many have more power than me. If we look at the story of Queen Esther, we are reminded that God *will* finish what He starts. Esther knows this. Confident and courageous, she is willing to risk everything to do what God asks of her. Esther knows something we all must learn: her life is not her own.

Beth Moore, a mentor to many through her in-depth Bible studies, recounts the various ways and things we fear as women: "What if... I die, he dies, my children die, I get cancer, we lose our money, he leaves me, I get divorced..."[1] The list goes on and on with endless possibilities. Fill in the blank for your circumstances. My fear, *this week*, is what if I do not get it all done? What if I do not complete what God started in me? There is too much to do and so little time. As a busy mom, I fear I will not impart to my daughters what I was called to impart and the time will pass too quickly. I fear I will miss it. Maybe I have a little FOMO (Fear Of Missing Out). Can you relate? I fear that I will die suddenly and will have left "too soon." My logical brain knows and believes God's Word in Philippians 1:6: "Being confident of this, that He who began a good work in you will carry it on to completion until the day of Christ Jesus." But my emotional brain thinks about my hairdresser who died tragically in a car accident on her way to Disneyland, my child's school friend who lost her mom to brain cancer, and the many husbands who are leaving their families because of addictions to pornography. The mind can go to endless possibilities and anxieties. The delayed text from my husband…did he die in a car accident? Letting my child go to a birthday party…will there be any child molesters there? Taking my child to school today…will she be bullied? Let's be honest—we all do this to some extent.

If you struggle with fear like I do, here are a few simple truths to remember. Living in a *constant* state of fear feels like a real waste of time and energy. In the long term, fear is not good for the body or the mind, but in short bursts it can be a helpful tool to keep us alert and prayerful.[2] In fact, God created fear, since He was the one who designed our entire beings, as a purposeful warning system. However, there are also many false alarms that go off in our bodies, especially in those who have unresolved trauma in their past. This is part of PTSD, or Post Traumatic Stress Disorder, where the brain stays in fight, flight, or freeze mode even in places of safety. This brain disorder is real, and treatment is available for it. (Many of my clients have seen incredible relief from their fear as their brains and bodies heal from their past.) Instead of allowing fear to isolate us, drive us to fight mode, or cause us to shut down, we can use fear to draw nearer to the Lord to find care and comfort in Him. Psalm 23 says, "The Lord is my shepherd, I lack nothing…he guides me along right paths for His name sake. Even through the darkest valley, I will fear no evil for you are with me." The presence of fear is not the culprit, but believing in its lies gives it power. Stay rooted in God's Word, which says that perfect love casts out fear (see 1 John 4:18).

As moms, our job is not to shelter our girls but to model and teach them how to trust God throughout their lives. A mentor in my life once told me there was not one prayer for protection throughout the book of Acts but rather prayers for boldness and courage. I was blown away by this idea and started praying for boldness and courage for my own girls. Both my girls have been known to stand up for kids at recess who are being teased or to share their faith in their public school with confidence. Teaching our girls to be sensitive to the Lord's leading and to trust Him with the consequences may require us moms to do the same. Knowing there is a greater purpose to our lives gives meaning to the courageous things we get to do in this life.

What do you fear these days? How are you leaning into God with all your might? I know that writing this book is one of the ways I am stepping out into faith instead of feeding my fears. I am not always certain if writing this book is for you or for me, but I am certain that it is the step I am meant to take in my own walk with God. It has taken years to get to this place in my own journey, and you are experiencing the fruit of something I never imagined would actually happen. But this book is a response to what has been birthed living in Christ, and His perfect love is casting out all my fear.

SHE IS RESILIENT

The prophet Jeremiah draws a powerful comparison between those who trust in the Lord and those who trust in their own strength. He says,

> This is what the Lord says: Cursed is the one who trusts in man, who draws strength from mere flesh and whose heart turns away from the Lord. That person will be like a bush in the wastelands; they will not see prosperity when it comes. They will dwell in the parched places of the desert, in a salt land where no one lives. But blessed is the one who trusts in the Lord, whose confidence is in him. They will be like a tree planted by the water that sends out its roots by the stream. It does not fear when heat comes; its leaves are always green. It has no worries in a year of drought and never fails to bear fruit. (Jeremiah 17:5-8, NIV)

Fear is a normal emotion in the human experience, and yet the Word tells us that when we are like a tree whose roots are deeply grounded by the streams, we do not have to fear hard times, troubles, or persecution. In fact, fruit will come forth from the life of one who trusts the Lord. Conversely, when we put our trust in ourselves, turning away from the Lord and drawing from our own strength, we are like a parched bush in a wasteland. As moms, where we place our trust and how we teach our girls to draw their strength can truly determine our resilience when life brings drought and heat. Preparing our daughters for the path, and not preparing the path for our daughters, is the most important principle we can learn.

In recent years, resilience has become a trendy word, but for good reason. It is only built through time and hardship. In the age of Amazon Now and Netflix binge-watching, it seems long-suffering and patience are hard to develop. Resilience is the ability to persevere and adjust when things go awry. Research shows that most people think they are resilient but are more at risk for giving up and feeling helpless than they realize. We are not born with resilience, but it is something we learn and develop. Some of the key factors of resilient people include an understanding that risk and failure are a part of the road to success. These people do not move away from challenges but understand how growth occurs as they face obstacles intentionally. Resilient people have anxieties and fears, but they have learned ways to cope with these emotions and have communities in place that help them find relief. The number-one factor for developing resilience is the way we make meaning of our world and interpret circumstances that happen to us outside of our control.[3] The difference between having power or feeling powerless can be as simple as the way we think.

Walking with some of the most resilient women and girls I know, I have learned a profound principle about God: He has made His people capable of moving through anything! Rebuilding, restoring, and renewing what we once thought was lost is God's primary business and is the work to which He calls His people. While not all things will be *fully* restored in this life, He is surely accomplishing a mighty work in the world, despite the way it might look to us as humans. One of our primary goals of raising girls must be to help them move through whatever difficulties life brings their way by teaching them to consider God and His ways in the midst of all of life's mess.

If we are quick to diminish hardship with typical and trite sayings, our daughters are at risk for becoming severely naive and vulnerable to the wolves of this world. Instead, let's equip them with the truth that empowers them to navigate life's trials. When we teach them that God uses all things for the glory of His children (see Romans 8:28), that doesn't mean we will always understand why certain things occur. We like to believe that if we do and say the right things, in the right order, then all will be okay. But the reality is, we cannot control most of what happens in this life. Believing otherwise is just a way to have a false sense of control or comfort ourselves, but it leaves us with a hangover that deflates our souls. In this reality, there is one thing we must hold onto: no matter the why behind what happens to us, we have choices on how we respond to our circumstances. Teaching our girls the power of choice in the face of diversity can be one of the greatest gifts we can ever give them.

SHE TRUSTS WHEN LIFE DERAILS

Life is unpredictable. Sometimes it takes us through twists and turns we feel unprepared to face: we receive a diagnosis; a child struggles in a way never expected; our spouse betrays us. Grief weaves a wide range of emotions, including sadness, anger, bargaining, and acceptance. Grief derails us, and the path of healing from the hardships of life is a continual process that never runs in a straight line.

Jay and Katherine Wolf recently shared their journey of a drastic life derailment and how a paradigm shift saved their lives. Newly married, Katherine had hopes of being a model while husband, Jay, was in law school. The big dreams of this young couple were coming true, including a shared love for their sweet six-month-old son. Life seemed to be going just as they had hoped and planned it would, until one day when Jay found his wife on the floor of their home. She was taken to UCLA hospital; they had no idea what lay ahead. That day, Katherine nearly died. Doctors warned Jay that, after suffering a massive brain stem stroke at the age of 26, her chances of surviving were slim. By a miracle, Katherine did survive. After two months, she came out of her coma.

As I sat in the audience of a crowded auditorium, listening to her harrowing story, I could hear a deep peace beneath Katherine's words. She shared that once she awoke she could tell that time had passed by the size of her sweet baby's thighs. They were much bigger now. Mentally, she tried to reach out to hold her young child, but her brain did not communicate with her arms. She was paralyzed. She could no longer hold her child, and devastation ached in every part of her body. My own maternal heart ached for her as I listened.

Now, ten years later, the Wolfs share their story in their book, *Hope Heals.* Now, their testimony holds deeper meaning, presence, and identity, beyond what they could have ever imagined prior to the stroke. Katherine still lives with many disabilities and has had to fight to regain basic functions, but their story is a must-read for anyone struggling to see beyond loss. Theirs is a story that presents an alternative to unexpected derailment: hopeful transformation. When they thought they had lost everything, the Wolfs say they actually found what they were missing all along.

In their book, Katherine and Jay share their redemptive story in the most authentic way. It is not just a story of a couple who managed to find the silver lining in crisis. In other words, it is more than an attempt to bring shallow, short-lived hope to dark places. Instead, it is an honest and true story about how deep, abiding restoration happens outside the lines of what we might initially imagine life looking like.

I recently met Jay and Katherine. Standing in their presence, I could see their confidence was in the Lord. Katherine, a Courageous Mama, is an example of a woman who would neither give up nor become bitter. In the depths of her greatest fears—never being the kind of mom she had wanted to be for her child—she heard God remind her of the truths she memorized as a young girl. At one point, she questioned if God made a mistake in keeping her alive. In that moment, she says,

> I feel a deep awakening of the Word of God, which I had known since I was a little girl. I could almost hear this rapid-fire succession of the truths of Scriptures, like a dispatch from God Himself.

Katherine, you are not a mistake. I DON'T MAKE MISTAKES. I know better than you know. I am God, and you're not. Remember that you were fearfully and wonderfully made in you mother's womb, and that is when the AVM formed in your brain. There is a purpose for all of this. Just wait. You'll see. There is no replacing you!....Trust Me. I am working out EVERYTHING for your good. Don't doubt this truth just because you are in darkness now. What is true in the light is true in the dark. I know you can't fight this. That doesn't matter. All you have to do is be still and let Me fight for you. I will complete the good work I began when I gave you new life. I will carry it on to completion. Believe that. My nature is to redeem and restore and strengthen. This terrible season will come to an end. You will suffer for a little while, and then I will carry you out to this. You will see My goodness in the land of the living. Lean into this hope. Let it teach you how special you are. Most people will never go through this kind of hell on earth. I have chosen you. Live a life worthy of this special calling you have received.[4]

Katherine's childhood was filled with learning the Word and building a relationship with the God of the universe so that in her moment of doubt He could download the truths of His heart into hers. If you are not familiar with the Bible, those words are a string of scriptures. Integrating God's Word throughout the CG curriculum imbeds our daughters' hearts with God's truth for moments when they desperately need reminding of His love and plan. I pray our Courageous Girls would not only know the depths of God's Word for whatever roads they go down in life, but that their relationship with Him is so secure that doubt only pushes them deeper in His presence.

Resilience and courage are not about being strong but about leaning into the One who is stronger than anything we could ever face. I have to remind my mama heart of this daily as I send my girls into the world. I actually had my oldest read *Hope Heals* as a means of dialoging with her about life's hardships and God's redemptive work. Healing does not always look like we want or think, but God does far more in it than we can imagine.

The theology of suffering is a topic moms do not want to consider much, let alone discuss with our daughters. Yet, we *are* teaching our daughters daily what we think about suffering when we respond to their wounds—whether smaller wounds from the *strict* teacher at school or the *mean* volleyball coach on the court, or bigger wounds from a recent divorce or racist comments at recess. The truth is, God never promised us a "good" life, free from troubles or trials. Instead, God said He would give us abundant life. Katherine is the kind of resilient woman I want to be and model to my girls. She reminds me that hope is a state of mind, not a destination. She did arrive at hope overnight, but in the process of shifting into a hope-centered mindset she found the diamonds in her story that now shine brightly in a dark world. The meltdowns about a missed parking spot or a bad-hair day have got to stop in my own life. How about in yours? Life tends not to go our way, and the practice of breathing deeply, talking to Jesus, and letting go of the belief that everyone else has it easier than us will strengthen us.

In years of ministry and counseling various populations, I have heard stories from every type of woman. Just when I think, *this woman has got it together,* I hear a little insecure girl tucked inside her that no one else can see. When we think that someone "has it all" or has not experienced suffering, we have been fooled by social media and the masks we try to wear. This woman does not exist, and owning this truth frees us up to have compassion for ourselves and others. Moms, we need to teach our girls the stories of the Bible when God does *not* answer prayers. Hebrews 11 is full of men and women of faith who never saw the ways in which God answered their deepest longings. Each of them had faith that God was working and would fulfill His promise, but it was generations before God completed what He started.

Now faith is being sure of what we hope for and certain of what we do not see. This is what the ancients were commended for. By faith we understand that the universe was formed at God's command, so that what is seen was not made out of what was visible. Hebrews 11:1-3 (NIV)

147

God does not always let us know what He is is doing; that is why our journey is one of faith. I often wonder how I show my girls faith in the tangible moments of life. Do they just believe that their laundry will get done and then *poof*...it magically appears all neatly folded in their closets? How are they learning resilience and growing their faith muscles as nine- and eleven-year olds? The only way I am able to answer that question is by evaluating the ways in which I let them struggle. And believe me, my Merchant mama heart does not like to see my babies struggle.

This attitude reminds me of a story. There once was a man who watched a butterfly struggling to emerge from a cocoon. After hours of exhausted effort, the man felt concern for the butterfly. In an attempt to help release the butterfly, he took scissors to the cocoon to launch the butterfly into nature. However, after he opened the cocoon, he realized that the butterfly had wrinkled and crumbled wings and could not fly. The man had failed to understand that the butterfly's struggle was necessary for it to develop stronger wings so that the butterfly could fly. In trying to "help" the butterfly, the man actually limited its abilities. As moms, we need to remember that we cannot cut our child's cocoon out of our compassion or heartbreak.

We have seen the result of this type of parenting in the Millennials (born 1983-2000), generally parented by baby boomers who did not want to see their children do without any material wants. Many Millennials grew up in dual-income homes where both parents were very busy working overtime. This left the average parent too exhausted to attend to their child's typical emotional needs and led to shortcut parenting. Instead of teaching their children the art of prolonged gratification and emotional regulation, Millennials were given what they wanted and handed smart phones as little children to avoid meltdowns. This has only become worse as Millennials become parents.[5]

We need to recover the resilience factor. We *can* help our daughters learn how to move through difficulties rather than around them. My parents gave me the gift of not rescuing me. I remember my sixth-grade state report. I had grand plans for my visual aid about the great state of Texas, my parents' home state. I procrastinated but was left with a choice: accept my project as unfinished or, slowly and steadily, finish what I started. My dad helped me understand the choice and my mom stayed by my side through my decision. I chose to finish what I started and my mom stayed up with me to help color in all the details I had so proudly drawn on my map. As the minutes ticked away and my tears flowed, her steady presence helped me persevere.

Every time I had a difficult situation in my home, my mom or dad would discuss my options with me and give me choices to make. Every difficulty provided a crossroad. This empowered me to think through the outcomes and to see the benefits of moving through rather than around. I am grateful for their foresight. They were preparing me for the road, and not the road for me. I am so grateful for their deep wisdom in this area of my life. It has created an inner strength and ability to assess my choices no matter what has come my way.

Courageous Mama, consider the ways in which you are practicing delayed gratification yourself, allowing your daughter to move through difficulties with hope. Resist the temptation to rescue her, and teach her how to reframe her frustrations as a means of growing muscles to fly. As you do so, do not leave her alone to figure it all out herself. Like my mom, who sat up with me late into the night, our girls need us to walk with them through the struggle. There is a time to protect our children, like when she wants to run into the street or jump off a propane tank, but we need to draw a line so as not to enable our children to appease our own fears. We have become scared of our girls and their momentary outbursts of emotions. They desperately need us to lead the way in our own lives. Choose what you will do with your circumstances. If it's helpful, lean into your husbands, who more often tend to avoid enabling and find it easier than us to encourage risk-taking. Take back your life from living in fear and allow God to use your story for His greater glory. He can. He will. He does.

Our daughters need to be equipped for an unkind world that will try to kill, steal, and destroy anything good in them. When we tell them the Disney messages to "follow their heart and their dreams will come true," we withhold from them the full truth and ignore the responsibility to help them deal with disappointment and heartache. The "American Idol syndrome," or fast track to success prosperity gospel, has invaded our churches and our parenting. We need to reassess if this is really the gospel message.

The Word says, "Delight in the Lord. He will give you the desires of your heart" (Psalm 37:4, NIV). Whether He changes our hearts to align with His purposes or He puts desires in our hearts that align with His purposes, the point is to delight in the Lord. Our girls will learn from us as we choose not to ignore or crumble but rather face our fears in the midst of darkness. One of my most treasured passages says, "Do not fear, for I have redeemed you; I have summoned you by name; you are mine. When you pass through the waters, I will be with you. When you pass through the rivers, they will not sweep over you. When you walk through the fire, you will not be burned; the flames will not set you ablaze. For I am the Lord your God, the Holy One of Israel, your Savior. I give Egypt for your ransom, Cush and Seba in your stead. Since you are precious and honored in my sight, and because I love you" (Isaiah 43: 1b-4a). These verses don't say, "If you pass through the waters…" but rather, "*When* you…" We *can* be courageous throughout life's storms, which are inevitable. If you need some encouragement for your soul in the midst of feeling fear, read all of Isaiah 43. Let its truths wash over you and bring hope. Pray it over your daughter and your home.

SHE KNOWS HOW TO CALM HER ANXIETIES

It is very important to remember that having anxieties and fears is *normal* and part of the human condition; emotions are not a surprise to God. That's why so many passages in scripture speak to them. God knows us and is not disappointed when we feel anxiety. He wants us to run to Him. It's like when our daughters get scared of the dark. For years I used a night light and reminded them that the light represented the Holy Spirit. He is present and penetrates the darkness. Meditating on Him, rather than our fears, is how we regulate these human responses. Christians are especially guilty of shaming these feelings as we tell each other that we "should not be anxious." That is neither helpful nor biblical. God created warning systems in our bodies for very clever reasons.

There is a difference between fear and anxiety. Fear is being afraid of something we know we do not like, for example, being afraid of spiders. Anxiety is the fear of the unknown. Both fear and anxiety produce chemical reactions in our body and activate our amygdala in our downstairs brain. The more trauma in our background, the faster the amygdala activates, sending our bodies into fight, flight, or freeze mode. On the other hand, the more time we spend time grieving and truly processing our story, the more our brains know how to rest.

Some of us have biological factors that impact our anxiety levels. Hormones, our genes, the foods we eat and what we spend our time meditating on impact the way our brains react to the world around us. In training and equipping ministry leaders, counselors, and business leaders, Jeff and I have gone as far as to say we think the digital age and the amount of violence available for viewing has changed the makeup of our brains. Today, we have larger populations of PTSD than ever before, especially among the Millennial and Now generations. Studies have shown that people can actually get PTSD just by watching a traumatic moment if they have any sense that it could happen to them.[6] This is informative as we consider the exposure our girls have in their digital devices as their brains develop. Watching the news first thing in the morning might not be the best thing for our own fears and anxiety. Reading a scary book or watching a scary movie right before bed might not be the best habit either. The habits we form around our daily routines affect how quickly we can calm ourselves. Digital devices have been clinically proven to increase anxiety and stress in our bodies. Paying attention to the ways in which we spend our time will help our girls choose the same. Consider how often you are using your phone, the level of social media you are consuming a day, and the amount of tragic news entering your home through the TV and Alexa. Looking at your biology, history, habits, and daily routines will help you effectively assess controllable factors that can be adjusted and lead to reduced anxiety and fear.

For others, learning to reframe fear and anxiety as a friend rather than a foe may be the way to peace. Fear and anxiety can help us assess the outside dangers in our lives and give us permission to set healthy boundaries. For example, ignoring fear as one walks down a dark alley at night is not a good idea. We want to teach our girls to listen to these emotions and then share them with their moms, dads, and God. Ignoring emotions can lead us into years of poor decisions. I call my healthy anxiety my "red flags." I have become accustomed to listening to my body; when I feel caution in my gut, I pause long enough to pray, seek counsel, and wait until I receive further clarity. Teaching our girls to do the same will help them navigate their emotions well, producing healthier choices over time. Burn out or physical break down can be classic examples of how ignoring our anxieties for extended times can cause greater damage to our human systems.

Normalizing fear and anxiety is a huge factor for helping our daughters become resilient, rather than avoidant or naive. This actually creates courage, because we stop having anxiety about anxiety. Seriously! Fear of our own and other's emotions can be half of the battle. There is no feeling through which we cannot move. That is true both clinically and Biblically. Coming up with ways we can calm ourselves is an important tool to pass onto our girls before they leave our homes. Practice is the key. In the CG curriculum, we spend years processing this concept in very tangible ways. My own personal five regulators are: 1) talking with others because I am a verbal processor; 2) journaling my concerns and reading scripture for Truth; 3) walking in nature as I engage all five of my senses - touch, smell, see, taste, and hear; 4) exercising, as it provides many feel good endorphins and releases stress; and 5) listening to music. Most girls do not know what to do in the midst of their fear and anxieties. We need five ideas at the tip of our fingers just in case one or two do not work! Sometimes we may need to do all five. Equipping our daughters with five — one for each finger on their hands — can make the difference between a momentary impulsive decision and seeking the help they need. Most girls do not know what to do in the midst of their fear and anxieties.

As we help our daughters navigate their emotions, it's important to remember the value of validating their emotions. The ACT model from the Play Therapy Parent Coaching model[7] suggests that validating our child's emotions, keeping good boundaries, and offering our children choices is a direct way to build resilience and self-regulation skills. We can start this at any age and continue through the teen years. "A" stands for acknowledging the emotion, "C" is for communicating the limit, and "T" is for targeting the alternative. An example could be when I find my free-spirited daughter running around barefoot in bee-infested land. She is feeling angst in her body and needs to run. I might say, "I know you have a lot of pent-up energy and need to run free. It feels good to be barefoot in the grass [A]. However, the bees might sting your feet, so you need to wear shoes outside while you run [C]. You can get your shoes now and continue running around, or you can run around barefoot inside. You choose [T]." This simple three-step process can keep us from controlling our children by helping us honor our girls' needs and emotions while also coaching them on how to make wise decisions. Affirming our children's God-given desires to explore and try new things, or be more cautious and discerning, is part of intentional parenting. When we set limits, they feel cared for, and when we provide alternatives, they feel powerful. God is good to do the same for us in His parenting.

Feeding our faith, building resilience, and learning how to calm our anxieties and fears are vital elements in the life of a Courageous Girl. Our daughters need to know that they can move through *anything* and that we will walk with them through the fire in their younger days. We do not rescue them but give them space to build the muscles so that they learn to fly.

Takeaway

Make a list of your top five fears. Next to each fear, write a truth statement from scripture or what you know to be true about yourself. Pray and ask God to give you opportunities to step out and practice faith. Then give God the credit when you see how He worked in and through you. Most of the time, if we look backward, we can be in awe of where we are today and how we have overcome through our stories. By God's grace, you are parenting a girl (or several girls) who is looking to you to teach her how to feed her faith, not her fears.

Read the book of Acts with other Courageous Mamas or with your daughter. Anytime you read the words "boldness," "courage," "power," study the context. Discuss the sort of danger described around or just before the disciples. Consider what fears you would feel if you were in their shoes? Notice what they pray for and how God answers their prayers. This will give you and your girls more biblical accounts to remember when your own fears arise.

Take It a Step Further

Write five ways you can calm your fears and anxiety. Fear and anxiety produce physical shifts in our body, so make sure at least one or two activities engage your body or senses with physical activities like cooking, knitting, walking, etc. Finally, write out five things you believe God is doing or will do in and through you. Feed your faith in a God who is able to do immeasurably more than we can ask or imagine (see Ephesians 3:20). Practice the ACT model with your daughter. When she finds herself in a difficult situation, acknowledge her emotions, communicate the limits, and target an alternative. Rather than reacting, watch her grow and develop her own sense of setting limits and making choices aligned with what she needs. Over time, she will lean toward you rather than becoming compliant or rebellious. You've got this, Mom—God is with you.

8

She Is His Beloved

I am my beloved's and my beloved is mine.
- **SONGS OF SOLOMON 6:3**

SHE THINKS CRITICALLY ABOUT CULTURAL NORMS

A Courageous Girl values her sexuality, a God-given and beautiful aspect of His design. The curriculum on the Courageous Girl's website is a proactive way we can help shape our daughters, and their view of themselves, in a world that tells them they are nothing more than a body to sell for someone else's pleasure. So many moms are fearful to talk "too early" to their daughters about this subject for fear they will awaken something inside their innocent little girls. Other moms operate from naïveté or ignorance because they have not given attention to developing their own healthy framework for God's good design for sex. If we are confused about what is true, healthy and normal sexuality, our confusion will interfere with our ability to parent well.

There is no shame in acknowledging we need help in this area. The enemy has worked really hard over generations to use sexuality as a means to kill, steal, and destroy. Please do not avoid reading this chapter, as it's written with grace and a deeper understanding of the many abusive and harmful ways we ourselves have been victims and persecutors of unhealthy sexuality. It might help you to read through this entire chapter first and then reread it to see which area God highlights to you. This topic may not be easy to approach, and your body might get triggered, but there is grace for all of us as we face our paradigms of sexuality and help our daughters do the same.

Our understanding of sexuality is shaped by a combination of our biology, experiences, education, and the unspoken rules of the culture in which we live. Culture is a broad term that can apply to a number of environments in which we find ourselves; our family, school, house of worship, city, country, as well as our ethnic and racial backgrounds all have cultural norms. Regardless of our stories, we all adopt the messages our communities pass (inadvertently or purposefully) to us. Pause to consider what you learned about sexuality in childhood and adolescent years. Your adulthood was likely a response to those learned lessons, but you may have had some additional trauma or healthy experiences that shape your views today. Many believe sex is either a gift, a god, or gross. Which word resonates with you the most? This may help you identify the voices of your sexual timeline.[1]

Sex and gender identity are at the core of many issues we face today as women and girls. The issue is so intertwined with our souls, and yet the courage it takes to discuss sexuality with our children keeps most parents from ever broaching the subject. In this chapter, I will share what I have learned listening to individuals and couples processing through sexual betrayal, addiction or childhood abuse. Those in my groups and in my office are teens, singles, married couples, people of faith, people not of faith, and everyone in between. These issues are quite complex, so please understand that I am not oversimplifying but rather asking moms to slow down and evaluate our concerns against the truth of God's Word and His plan for our lives.

I have never met a woman who has not been impacted by the cultural sexual shift that has recently taken place. This shift toward "rape culture" has created an environment where girls no longer recognize the subtle and devaluing messages about our sexuality. "Rape culture" is such a harsh phrase, but both sacred and secular experts have named this condition as they analyze music, media, social structures, universities and work places of our times.[2] The recent outpouring of women stating "me too" on social media should be enough to show that it is time to stand up against the shift toward violence against and sexualization of women in every aspect of our culture.

Healthy sexuality, from a clinical and biblical worldview, produces healthy brains, healthy relationships, and healthy family systems. *Girls & Sex,* by intelligent and well-respected journalist Peggy Orenstein, is one of the most validating books I have read on this subject. Orenstein has no agenda but to explore the impact of current culture and how it shapes the way girls view and engage in their sexuality. Peggy explores the impact of pornography and social media, pointing out how the "selfie generation" has transformed talking about one's self as an individual developing from within to a "brand" that should be marketed, bought and consumed.[3] Women at large are feeling the slow shift that has redefined what it means to be a woman and what it means to be sexually healthy. It's not just our daughters who are confused by these cultural shifts. How can we help our daughters when we are buying into the lies as well?

Orenstein bravely put into words what hundreds of interviews revealed on the realities girls are facing today. She spoke with girls regarding their self-identified sexual identities. Many of the girls interviewed had done Internet searches on whether they are transgender, gay or bi-sexual based on a dislike for "girl" norms like dance classes, wearing makeup, or wearing feminine clothing. Relying on Google for answers around questions of sexual identity can become life-altering. Orenstein responds with this profound statement: "When we've defined femininity for their generation so narrowly, in such a sexualized, commercialized, heteroeroticized way, where is the space, the vision, the celebration of other ways to be a girl?" Though Peggy and I might take different stances on why girls struggle and how they might make sense of their identify formation, we both agree that being a girl is defined too narrowly.

Growing up with a dad who *originally* wanted boys but eventually saw the delight of raising daughters, as a child I found myself identifying more with activities that men enjoyed. I was quite capable of keeping up with my male peers. I out-benched the football players during my freshman body-building class. I could not wait to run home and brag to my dad (who still tells the story today). I did not want to be a part of "girl drama." I did not wear much makeup, and I avoided painting my

157

nails to avoid being too girlie. I was a tomboy for years and preferred a more natural look. If I grew up with the messaging of today and had the Internet to do a search, I might have questioned my gender identity. I cannot know for sure, but I do know that because I grew up prior to the "gender revolution" we find ourselves in today, the idea was never planted in my mind. The cultural norm in my world was that being a girl was broad enough so that I could be both strong *and* a girl. Despite the attempts, the "expanding definitions" of our day actually seem to be narrowing our gender perspectives. We are too quick to define our children and let them discern their own sexuality and gender identity. From a neuroscientific and human developmental point of view, a third-grader is not ready to make those kinds of decisions, though it is becoming a more common and accepted norm. We would not let her or encourage her to choose a mate, a career, or drive before she's ready, so why would we encourage her to decide if she is male or female?

God ordains each person with purpose. In that purpose, He provides a lot of freedom with a few boundaries. I happily identify as a woman. In my twenties, I wrestled with what it means to be feminine. I have since embraced wearing makeup, accessorizing, and shopping, all stereotypically feminine things. But I'm still a business owner, coach, consultant and teacher of men and women. I like being strong. I'm not sure I can out-bench any men today, but I do help my husband lift and move heavy objects on our property regularly. Being physically strong has come in handy! My husband might miss the more "natural' woman he fell in love with, since our household budget has absorbed some of the habits I have picked up over the years, but I'm proud that I can still throw a football and gut my own fish.

When we try to construct an identity for ourselves, we will ultimately feel amiss. The thirst in our souls will remain. We are very confused people, on all issues, and this is why we need direction from our Creator. Please, hear my heart; my views are not based on theoretical circumstances. I have sat and considered the issues of sexuality in the most personal ways, from the effects of sexual abuse, sexual betrayal, gender identity, premarital sex, sex trafficking, and more. I have walked with real people and have chosen to join them where they are, in the center of their pain, with compassion. In the written form, these topics can sound trite and merely cognitive. But I have tied my very being to these words. For most of my forty years, I have been faced with these issues in my family-of-origin, friendships, community, ministry, and professional counseling experience. I am not claiming to be an expert on this topic, but I might know a little more than the average mama.

SHE VALUES BOTH MALE AND FEMALE CONTRIBUTIONS

Questioning our sexuality is ultimately about finding our identity and purpose. "Who I am meant to be" is a complex question and must be explored over time, in relationship and with careful consideration of the Word. A teenage girl who is not sexually aroused by her boyfriend pressuring her to explore his body should not wonder if she's a lesbian. Similarly, a woman who is often disgusted by her sexual relationship with her husband, who is addicted to porn and exhibits no emotional intimacy, need not question her identity. The young girl who is excited that her female friend might have a crush on her, particularly if this relationship is the only place she has found love, attention, and human connection, does not have cause to question her sexual orientation. In all these areas, guided coaching is needed more than an exploration of sexual orientation.

Our sexuality is partly influenced by our biology and mostly influenced by life experiences and cultural influences. When I was a girl, I would hold hands with my best girlfriends. It felt safer to dance with them at the eighth-grade dance than with the boys. (Let's be honest, the boys were quite stinky and awkward.) Girlfriends are better in so many ways when we are growing up, at least until boys move beyond their hormonal shifts and start to mature. It's no secret that we are feeling the "The Great Demise of Guys"[4] due to the "Digital Invasion."[5] Boys lack social skills more than ever before, and our girls are desperate for someone to look them in the eyes. Guiding our girls through all the experiences, questions, exposure, and inward processing is a powerful, needed, and sacred gift of being a mom.

Gender matters. Though this book is about girls, we must include a little information about boys when exploring these subjects. The Bible is not the only literature that says gender matters. In the age of gender fluidity, it's important to speak to the glaring biological evidence that science still supports key differences between males and females. Our predetermined chromosomes and genitalia are not the only defining factors, though the current popular thought might claim differently. Researcher, psychologist and pediatrician Leonard Sax, MD, PhD, brings this to the forefront when he says, "Male testosterone washes over the male brain in utero, creating a variety of distinct differences. This particular hormone is responsible for higher risk-taking, less self-control, and competitiveness. Each male has a varying level of this hormone, which may explain the differences and variables between boys. However, in general, teachers and parents should consider the biological differences as they engage these little ones. Quickly diagnosing boys with behavioral problems and disorders can be dangerous (though appropriate at times), as many boys are just living out of their brain design and have been increasingly impacted by the level of digital engagement. From early on, studies show that boys have more learning and disciplinary issues than girls and we can attribute these higher statistics to their key brain development."[6] Though boys are part of God's amazing design, our boys are struggling on a greater systemic plain. Raising boys who not only value women but also see their God-given design is a huge calling and may be addressed at some point in another book.

If we consider the ways in which males and females are created from birth, we can better understand their day-to-day interactions at home, school, and work. Hearing and smelling senses are more acute in females, making a middle school girl more likely to hear a teacher's instructions and be turned off by a boy's body odor, and making a mother more "sensitive" to the voices of her children calling when she is trying to have a romantic moment with her spouse. These biological factors impact many aspects of how we relate to our world. When a husband does not hear his wife's words the first time, could it be because his hearing does not pick up the same frequencies as a woman? When a son has a hard time settling down after a long day at school, could it be because he just needs a change of environment where he can exert physical energy, compete, and take risks? Considering the science on gender can help us attune to better solutions for our relational mishaps.

The greater challenge for our society, according to Jonathan Haidt, a social psychologist at New York University Stern School of Business, is to help boys become men who are committed to supporting women and children, since their biological bent toward independence and adventure can keep them from nurturing relationships.[7] The "Great Demise of Men" refers to the idea that fewer men are going to college, committing to marriage, and leaving Mom and Dad's couch to earn a living. This reality is partly due to addictions to pornography and over-sexualization in our culture. But it also may be due to devaluing what maleness innately brings to furthering our human race and how it reflects God's character. Women's response to years of oppression has been to turn the tide and make men feel inferior. You may not agree, but look around. You will easily find women saving men in movies, making fun of men on sitcoms, and reducing men with the casual side comment "They only want one thing." When we devalue men, we contribute to their "great demise."

Let's pause and consider why this matters in raising our daughters to be courageous. How we view men, talk about men, raise our boys, and treat our husbands helps our daughters choose to value men and boys as well. Our words, actions, and subtle responses can lead our girls to see males as part of God's plan, not to be feared, ignored or dismissed. When Courageous Girls learn about God's value and purpose for them, they will be able to identity the counterfeits. They will neither seek men for their identity and worth nor treat men with disrespect or disregard. It's all integrated in this greater systemic shift we long to see. We have come so far in valuing women over the years, but the pendulum swing might have gone too far. It is important to consider our own biases, stories, and cultural norms around gender roles, stay educated on the current data, and funnel everything through the lens of scripture as we teach our daughters to live out of who God designed them to be.

SHE IS EDUCATED ON THE RELEVANT ISSUES

In an age when we are moving from a binary culture (male and female) to a pluralistic culture (with 66-200 gender types), we cannot lose sight of the science of gender. Be educated moms. Gender statistics have not really changed, though our interpretation of the evidence may be changing. God created male and female as a beautiful reflection of the triune God (see Genesis 1:27). Personally, I believe the design of male and female is a beautiful thing. The collaboration of the two genders can breed a powerful challenge, rounding out our humanity, causing us to think and live outside of our own nature. Moving beyond ourselves is a growing opportunity for all of us and takes daily practice. For a single mom, hanging out with other couples and having male friends can be a powerful way to model to your girls that not all men are unsafe, unkind, and "only after one thing." One gender without the other can feel lopsided because it only reflects part of our triune God's nature.

The evidence of gender research reveals that most girls are more relationally aware than boys and have more complex responses to their environments. They have brains that are more integrated and allow more access between the emotional and logical brain. Due to the brain development of men, most are focused on one thing at a time and therefore can compartmentalize more easily. Both of these tendencies have purpose and work beautifully in tandem. Letting go of our identities as male and female can become a slow departure from the truth of science and, in a way, like the clay pot telling the potter that he made a mistake. Becoming educated on our children's, spouse's, and colleagues' unique gender differences can open our eyes to the wonder of how we can partner together.

I have helped people in their search for healthy sexuality for twenty years. At the core of both men and women is a longing to be known, loved, significant and accepted. We keep trying to meet our legitimate needs in illegitimate ways. Seeking only the orgasm, the romantic experience, or the high-intensity dopamine fix has created social epidemics and cultural addictions. This mind-set has infused its way into all our daily habits, whether we like it or not. We have to stand up and lead our girls. It is not good leadership to leave them to discern their own sexuality, the way they present their bodies to the world, or try to experiment in order to discover their identity and purpose in life.

The Hawaiian-themed Disney movie *Moana* has an amazing scene at the end. Moana is called to restore the heart to a lava monster, Te Ka, which had been stolen long ago by the demi-god Maui. As many Disney princesses do, Moana sings to Te Ka and bravely faces her fire-throwing anger. In singing, "This is not who you are. We know who you are," she successfully restores Te Ka's heart. The lava, Te-Ka's primary defense, subsides, and Te Ka's true beauty is revealed. It gets me every time!

This is our call: to remind our girls, our boys, ourselves, other moms, our husbands, and the world around us, "This is not who you are; we know who you are." Humans are not brands to be sold, used or minimized as body parts. We are not meant to give of ourselves so intimately in such shallow and casual ways. The gift of sex has been turned into a dirty tool to use and has lost its meaning.

Being confused and disoriented about gender identities, roles, and expressions of our sexual nature are not new things. It is an age-old issue for humanity, and God's ways have brought clarity time and time again. We can read story after story in the Old and New Testaments about the variety of ways God's people struggled to regulate their sexuality or even used sexuality to cause great devastation. (To name a few: Genesis 19 & 38; Leviticus 18 & 20; 2 Samuel 11 & 13; Judges 19:22; Romans 1.) Sex has been reduced to gratifying lustful pleasures or performing duty. Because of this, we should not be surprised when those outside the church make sex the central issue. Several of the epistles constantly warn the church against this practice. The church in Corinth provides a classic example of how the church integrated cultural norms into ecclesial practices, and Paul makes it very clear that these behaviors were unacceptable according to God's ways (see 1 Corinthians 5:1-2). As we help our daughters walk through questions of gender, sexual identity and healthy partnership between males and females, we must remember God's perspective. The human ways have drawn us astray, but when we trust in the Lord and in all our ways acknowledge Him and His ways, He will make our path straight (see Proverbs 3:4-5).

SHE ADDRESSES SEXUALITY WITHOUT SHAME

Sexual relationships were originally designed for six reasons: to create a unique bond between a husband and wife, to provide comfort, to enjoy pleasure, to create life, to reflect intimate knowing, and to express life-long commitment.[8] Sex was designed as the expression of our love for one another. The beautiful picture calms many of our hearts as we consider the purpose behind the design. The enemy and the selfish ways of humanity have tainted its value.

There is deep and rich theology around sexually intimacy. Sadly, many churches rarely teach it correctly. Women either use sex to keep their husbands satisfied or from being unfaithful. Many have full distain for the act. Teens and girls use sexuality as a means to get love and attention. We are trying to find love in all the wrong places. These oversimplified examples are not to minimize the issues but to help us see what lies beneath the surface for most of us. Sex has become a dreaded topic for many moms, and their daughters' uncomfortable responses might dictate the conversations needed along the road of life.

Hear, O Israel: The LORD our God, the LORD is one. You shall love the LORD your God with all your heart and with all your soul and with all your might. And these words that I command you today shall be on your heart. You shall teach them diligently to your children, and shall talk of them when you sit in your house, and when you walk by the way, and when you lie down, and when you rise. You shall bind them as a sign on your hand,

and they shall be as frontlets between your eyes. You shall write them on the doorposts of your house and on your gates. Deuteronomy 6:4-8 (ESV)

We cannot expect our girls to know or understand how to live out loving God with all our heart, soul and might if we do not model and address sexuality as women. This includes acknowledging our changing bodies and sexuality. If we do not lead our girls, the world will. Saying nothing about our sexuality can speak louder than our words. When we speak vaguely, we leave open holes for others to fill. There is a process of talking with our girls at appropriate developmental stages, equipping them to understand and appreciate their uniquely female bodies. In the context of safe conversations, we also need to give them a foundation for God's profound design for sex, which passes on a passion for purity before and during marriage. (Keeping the marriage bed pure, according to Hebrews 13:4, applies to before and after the wedding.) The Courageous Girls curriculum was designed to help us tackle these difficult topics at each stage of life. Moving toward such conversations around biological changes, crushes, dating, gender identity, and pornography allows us to "normalize" a daughter's curiosities and help calm her nerves about these subjects, reducing her chance of falling prey to another person's agenda. Knowing biblical and clinical truths about the matter can help her have a voice, say no and get help if she is ever in a situation where she could be violated.

Talking about sex is not just to help our daughters avoid being a victim to offenders. Sex touches something deep in our soul. We have tried to turn that lever off in order to be seen in a culture that over-sexualizes, but it has not worked. Let's consider how out of balance we have become regarding sexuality, gender and body-image issues. These statistics are always changing, and I fear that by the time this book is in print they will be outdated and even more extreme. Fifty percent of girls in middle school have tried oral sex. By the time a girl is sixteen, 60 percent have had intercourse with at least one person. By the time a girl graduates from college, she is likely to have experienced one form of sexual assault or sexual abuse, regardless of her background.[9] A recent study conducted by the Harvard Graduate School of Education found that 87 percent of women aged 18-25 years old reported having experienced sexual harassment in their lifetime; only 24 percent had ever talked with their parents about how to avoid these situations.[10] One in three girls is sexually abused by a "trusted" person in her life. One in two girls thinks her "ideal" body weight is less than she actually weighs.[11] Every girl has been affected by the cultural norms of being "pretty." Self-harming behaviors such as cutting, eating disorders, pornography addictions, and even suicide are at the highest rates ever in many age groups and are rising still. The average girl is first exposed to pornography between the ages of 8 and 11 years old.

The reality is that the sex and pornography industries are looming over our homes, destroying our marriages, and teaching our children that we are merely animals driven by our uncontrolled visceral and primal needs. We spend billions on beauty products, gym memberships, and buttocks reconstruction—for what? So that we will be loved? So that we will be seen? So that someone will notice our beauty and fulfill our longing to be cherished?

Mamas—let's get these statistics into our heads! Tear away the veil of indifference and the comforting mantras ("that's not my daughter") that we replay in our heads. The daughters of many good mamas have been in my counseling office telling me things she believed she could not tell you. In those moments, I desperately wanted *you* to be the one to help her. That is the original design for parenting. You can be her greatest advocate and guide. She is watching you! If we do not actively participate in processing these issues at a developmentally appropriate pace, the culture will surely beat us to the punch!

SHE PLACES SEX IN ITS RIGHTFUL PLACE

Let us finish this chapter with discussing a healthy view of sexual intimacy from both a biblical and clinical worldview. Counterfeit detectives confess that when they study the authentic dollar bill in-depth, they are able to spot the fake one faster. This principle can be applied all over the place, especially in the realm of healthy sexuality.

Sex, in its rightful place within the context of marriage, is like eating dessert: it is meant to be the end of a nutritious meal, not the main course. Using sex as the means for any couple to sustain a life-long connected marriage is like living on dessert. Sex is meant to add to the greater enjoyment within the relationship, not be the focus. Grandma Bowery always said, "Eat dessert first," which has become a fun tradition our family has adopted, and my children relish it on special occasions. (In fact, I just took my youngest out for ice cream before we ventured to dinner. We both giggled as we delighted in our treats!) But we all know that, even though it's exciting to eat dessert first, it can spoil our dinner and leave our bodies with unintended side effects in the long haul. If we ate this way on a regular basis, our bodies would have all kinds of negative symptoms, such as heart disease, diabetes and low energy. Sex is intended to be enjoyed when a husband and wife have invested in the hard work of preparing and digesting emotional intimacy, commitment, and shared meaning. Otherwise experienced, such as in premarital sex or as the only means of expressing love in a marriage, sex will become detrimental to one's spiritual, emotional, and relational health.

Sex is something worth waiting for. Many of us adults express our own concerns for having sex too early in our lives or not knowing the long-term negative effects of premarital sex. Messages like "just don't" or "if you do, use protection" offer little help. Various forms of viewing sex in movies or pornography, or learning from experience, have been the main teacher for most. Some mamas project their own painful stories on their girls, not telling them the regret-filled mistakes made and how they would have lived differently if they had a second chance. While words may not be expressed, daughters can feel the shame that leaks from their mother's unresolved past. Another approach for mamas has been the "holier than thou" attitude, making daughters feel shame for even having a desire for sexual pleasure. The truth is that God created us as sexual beings; our lesson is to learn how to relegate our sexuality to its rightful place. Just like our emotions, food appetites and spending habits, regulating and making wise choices that leave us feeling whole and not harmed are the keys to health.

As I have processed sexuality at every level, the root of the issue for all people always comes down to a longing for authentic connection and emotional intimacy. Using sex as a means to escape, cope, get or keep love, find value, or define ourselves are all harmful ways of relating to sex and will lead us to a dead end. Sex is meant to be the *result* of deep emotional intimacy, not the producer of it. When sex is brought into a relationship prior to marriage, in any form, there are damaging effects. Our sexuality is reinforced by whatever we have been exposed to: pornography, abuse, promiscuity, shame, spiritual legalism, and so forth. Similar to smoking, the risk for lung cancer is much higher for one who smokes than for those who do not. Protecting and honoring our bodies and their intended sexuality is a means to a healthier sexual relationship in marriage. We can talk to our girls about purity and premarital sex within this context. Here is what relationship and sexual-formation experts know:

1. Women want to be chosen. When sex is simply an act of ecstasy, orgasm, and reduced to a momentary pleasure, it produces a feeling of objectivity.

2. Relationships where sexual boundaries were honored and respected prior to marriage have higher levels of trust than in relationships where the boundaries were crossed.

3. When someone can regulate their sexuality prior to marriage, which simply means they will not give into its every craving, they are a more likely candidate for faithfulness in marriage.[12]

4. Monogamy produces the greatest satisfaction in sex and overall relationships than any other sexual relationship.

5. When our "no, thank you" is honored in the sexual relationship, our "no, thank you" is honored in all parts of the relationship. Boundaries are crossed in all areas of a relationship when one partner is unable to hear "no" to their needs and wants. It's like

a two-year-old who wants a cookie. If she can't hear "no" now, she won't hear it when she's a teenager.

6. Sex is one of the most intimate acts, though it has been diluted by our culture to what a wave or handshake used to mean. Nowadays, one does not need to know another well to have, or be committed past, a physical encounter. The ironic thing is that scripturally, "Adam *knew* his wife" is the same Hebrew word for God *knowing* us. The terms are synonymous in the original language. This has huge implications for the intent of sex, the spiritual connection it can create, and the vulnerability it requires. Engaging in sex without vulnerability and emotional intimacy requires great dissociation from our hearts, minds, and bodies.

7. Sex offers us a huge dose of oxytocin (a body-agent hormone) and dopamine (a "feel good" hormone). Oxytocin is the same hormone produced between a nursing mom and her baby so that they form an attachment. When applied in casual relationships, we are messing with the neuropathways in our brains that are trying to make healthy connections. The dopamine fix is meant to keep us coming back to each other. When used in combination, sexual intimacy can help us to feel closer and allow us to enjoy a precious gift with the most intimate person in our lives. I think God was pretty clever to make this the final step in our "consummation" of marriage. When you have committed to another person in covenant, then you bond with them.

8. Any sexual act that is connected to our "private" areas, or what we would cover with our bathing suit, is considered part of the sexual experience. I might hug another man and give my father a kiss on the cheek, but as a married woman, I would not engage in any other type of physical behavior with another male. This can help us define what is unacceptable outside of marriage when a girl asks how far she can go. Behaviors like sending photos, touching body parts, long kisses, petting, and even oral

sex can be justified by many but should be of concern when we teach our girls to value their bodies and their sexuality.

9. In unhealthy circles, women are told they should not withhold sex from their husbands because sex is the way her husband feels loved. The truth is that men must learn how to love outside of sex and to regulate their sexuality in order to honor their wives. First Corinthians speaks to both marriage partners. The wife does not have authority over her own body but yields it to her husband. In the same way, the husband does not have authority over his own body but yields it to his wife (see 7:4). This is a reflection of the divine dance. If both are giving, then there is safety and respect. If one seeks their own pleasure without consideration of the other, or seeks their needs outside of the relationship, then he or she truly misses the essence of design.

God's design was for men and women to give to and serve one another. In some cases, giving to your husband by making sex quick can be helpful for both partners. In other cases, saying "no, thank you, but let's try again this weekend" is a helpful approach that gives honor and respect to ourselves. The truth is, a husband will not die without sex, contrary to some popular teachings. I can promise that. It is up to a husband (or wife) to regulate their sexuality outside of masturbation, pornography or annoying the other spouse until they say yes.[12] Self-gratification is not the purpose of sex. Sex was created for a husband and wife to express mutual sacrifice in the context of a committed life-long relationship and for both partners' enjoyment, exploration, and edification.

In my office or at workshops, I often hear the question "Would you buy a car before you researched it?" Depending on your wiring, you may spend months on end comparing consumer reports, visiting various dealers, conducting test drives, and checking the engine with a professional. Having sex before marriage is similar to signing on the dotted line and buying a car prior to doing the homework needed for the purchase. The neurobiological and theological reasons for sex are that it is meant to bond us and create life. This amazing act is meant to be the celebration *after* all the research (praying, seeking counsel, having others give feedback) and demonstrated consistent track record. Do the hard work to explore who a person is, marry them, and *then* enjoy the gift of sex.

In summary, waiting to have sex until after marriage helps to establish trust, self-regulation skills, and fidelity. In a broader sense, it helps partners practice how to love and solve conflict outside of sex, which demonstrates that our inherent worth extends beyond what we do for each other. Hopefully by the time we choose to marry someone, we are also ready to parent a child, which is an obvious side effect of sexual intercourse. This kind of commitment requires a larger meaning and purpose than "because the Bible tells me so." Contrary to what many hope or believe, having sex before marriage does not lead to a happy and healthy relationship. If you have crossed those lines already, there is still hope, and we will address this later in the book.

SHE CHOOSES AND IS CHOSEN

Knowing and exercising one's voice, as well as making God-empowered choices, are pivotal aspects of a Courageous Girl. A valuable example of this is the act of being chosen *and* choosing who we date, who we marry, and who we engage sexually. While it may seem this aligns with the cultural norm, "I determine my destiny," it actually runs counter to that message. Biblical choice is rooted in a deep truth communicated again and again in God's Word that we are loved and can have intimacy with God and others outside of sex. Sex is not the means to "intimacy," and the desire for intimacy takes different forms in men and women. No matter how strong they are, all girls want to be protected, pursued, and cherished. No matter how passive some might be, all men want to protect, cherish, and pursue. This may feel outdated or archaic, but from the data in my office, this has continually proven to be true.

There is so much to say about sexuality, but for the sake of helping mamas and daughters, let's consider some practical ways we can integrate the value of our daughter's body and practice what it feels like when her "no" is respected. Teaching and practicing how to honor our bodies, even in the ways we care for it practically, establishes a firm foundation for healthy sexuality and body image in the teen and adult years. This helps our daughter defend against those who want to harm her both in and outside of close relationships. Initiating dialogue on these subjects with our daughter in her earliest developmental years is the best way we can help her. Here are some other practical ways we can help her value her body and respect her no.

1. Did you know that research has shown that healthy tickle games with our daughters develop confidence, resilience, intimacy, and other wonderful relationship skills? Starting from the beginning, many of us play tickle games with our girls. When they say "stop," we stop. Then, we say out loud, "I respect your no." So many in the world will not respect our no. If we are being honored in our homes, we will learn to set clear boundaries for ourselves. Otherwise, we will normalize crossing boundaries through simple games like tickling.

2. Around age 3 or 4, we can help our daughter learn to value her special body by encouraging her to shut the door when she goes to the bathroom. Talk about who can help her wipe, take a bath, or get her dressed. Limit this to safe people and explain that her special parts (those covered by her bathing suit) are for the bathroom and cleaning. As she ages, you will discuss other purposes for those special areas. Talk about good touch (such as wanted hugs, cuddling, holding hands), and bad touch (such as hitting, touching privates as a child, or not respecting someone's no). This also means not forcing your daughter (or children) to kiss Uncle John or get a hug from the teacher. Our cultural norms and the need to be "polite" can quickly override the greater and most needed message that people are to respect our no. This also means that showing or taking baths with siblings, cousins, or anyone else beyond the age of

two can become very confusing, and it's important to consider the cost in light of the inconvenience of bathing your children separately or skipping a bath if necessary.

3. When your daughter is changing, without a shameful tone or condemning body language, remind her that her body is special, and she can change in private. Changing in public spaces in the home and running around naked (developmentally, gender awareness begins between age two and three) can be confusing if we think about the greater vision for our girls. Remember, modesty without shame, value beyond our bodies, and using our voice to remain safe and within our God-given power and control will help your daughter to build confidence in who God designed her to be. This type of norm becomes natural as your daughters use the restroom at school, change in locker rooms, and go to other people's homes. She will have her own discernment to value her special parts and learn tricks to change, but recognize it's not because she needs to fear being sexualized, but rather because her body is not just for anyone. This takes lots of practice, ongoing dialogue, answering real-life questions throughout all the stages of life, and continuing to do our own work around our sexual paradigm.

4. Modesty, an issue we address in Courageous Girls curriculum at every developmental stage, varies from home to home. The most basic issues include talking about what we are wearing and the motive behind why we are wearing it. It is very important to teach our daughters that it is not their job to keep every boy and man from lusting after them by wearing a turtleneck or swimming in our clothes. Remember, the Bible teaches men (and women) to regulate their own sexuality in a way that it does not rule them. Modesty is "having or showing a moderate or humble estimate of one's merits, importance, etc.; free from vanity, egotism, boastfulness, or great pretensions."[13] This sounds pretty biblical to me. Often, today's outfits are intended to "show off" a physical asset we were given. The cultural message is, if you have them (breasts, tight abs, cute buttocks,

long legs, etc.), you should flaunt them. What does that mean when we do not like our bodies? In either case, using clothes to find our worth leaves us feeling empty. Our dress can be a form of expressing our creativity, meeting a practical need for comfort, or preparing for the task at hand. Showing off our private parts is not one of the main intentions, and talking about this with our girls, even when they are little, can help them own their sense of discernment. By late elementary school, taking your daughter shopping and inviting her to think through these issues with you will only add to her own sense of worth and enjoyment of clothes.

5. Let your girls practice letting someone open the door for them. Intentionally talk to them about how boys should treat them. We often pause TV shows, movies, and songs to talk through the messages that are being promulgated. Is that girl being valued? Is that boy treating her with respect? Recently, my family watched *Back to the Future*, a movie my husband and I used to love. We completely forgot that, in the movie, there is a scene where the main bully tries to sexually assault a girl. There was very little shown in the movie, but we paused and immediately discussed what it means when a boy is treating a girl that way. We asked whose fault it was (his, of course), and questioned what could the girl do. Left alone, our girls could have drawn a variety of conclusions. Given that sexual aggression has become so "normal," our girls need to know that a man should treat her with love, kindness and respect, and will honor her no! The moment he does not, he is no longer the man for her.

6. Continue to give your daughter choices in her daily routines (within reason). When she is age two, let her choose if she wants the apple sauce or the pear. When she is five, let her choose if she wants to wear the blue shirt or the red shirt. Choices start small, and they grow as our daughters grow. Making every decision for your daughter will only cause one of two things: (1) a girl who needs to be controlled and attracts controlling relationships, or

(2) a rebellious spirit who will go right when you suggest left. Choices come in all shapes and sizes, but working out our own sense of pride and emotional needs through our daughters can scar them for life. As parents, we need to provide limits (as God does for us), because this models greater principles for life.

Let me end with a real-life example. My nine-year-old daughter has a sense of style and picked out a pretty cute outfit. I can trust her ability to coordinate her outfits and discern how she feels in her clothes. It was a rushed morning (I am sure you can relate), and it was time to get in the car. I told her, "Grab your shoes and hop in the car." I did not think twice until she was stepping out of the car to walk into school, and I looked down to see her wearing her "outdoor chicken coop" boots. In my surprise, I exclaimed, "You wore your boots?" She looked back at me with a lowered brow and a sense of shame on her face. At that moment, I knew she was embarrassed and likely confused. I was ultimately concerned about her carrying chicken poop throughout the school hallway more than I was concerned about how she looked. This was what I communicated, and she immediately responded, "I thought I was supposed to wear shoes for the after-school playdate at our friend's farm." *Hmmm, good point,* I thought. In that split second, I had a choice. I could continue to feel my own embarrassment and shame of letting my daughter deliver fertilizer all over the school or recognize the greater opportunity to let my daughter have power in her own world. (Honestly, they were not the cutest pair of shoes with her oh, so cute outfit, so the decision was even harder.) I chose to honor her decision, by the help of the Holy Spirit, and owned my tone. It does not always go that way, but I followed up with her after school to make sure she knew that she was not in the wrong and encouraged her to think through her choice next time.

Choices are woven in every part of our lives, including parenting. They do not always directly relate to sexuality, but let me relay this as clearly as I can: the messages we learn about our power and control in our world will directly impact the kind of relationships we attract, the motives for our sexual behavior, and the ways we illegitimately use our bodies to gain what was once lost.

Courageous mama, I am for you. God is for you. And you *can* do this. Your daughter needs you, and it is never too late to start moving toward health. Lord, help us to "do all things through Christ who strengthens us" (Philippians 4:13). Amen!

Takeaway

If you have not addressed your own sexual story, recognize that may interfere with your ability to parent your daughter well. Start by creating a sexual timeline[14] and naming the lessons you have learned about your sexuality and gender identity through your own life experiences. Consider asking a professional, trusted friend or mentor to come alongside you and start processing your own pain. You are not alone. Until we grieve, forgive, and receive the grace offered us, our past will haunt us like a person buried alive; you never know when it will come up and try to grab your leg! It's an awful depiction, but that's the point! You are courageous. Addressing your story will give you the greatest advantage to help your daughter(s).

Take It a Step Further

Evaluate your daughter's age, and assess the needs she might have in her developmental stage. Go to the list above and discern which practice you want to integrate this month. Look for opportunities to discuss body care, modesty and the messages in your community about sexuality. Answer any of her questions. Normalize this type of conversation. If you are doing the Courageous Girls curriculum with a group of other moms, make sure you lean into them for prayer and wisdom.

9

She Dreams...Big

Jesus comes to people and invites us to be what-if people. He said to his early followers, "I want you to imagine a kingdom—the real magic kingdom. Imagine a kingdom where the last are first, the least are greatest, the servants are heroes, the weak are strong, and the marginalized are loved and cherished. Imagine a world where outsiders become insiders, where people who lose their lives end up finding them, where people who die to themselves and their guild and their sin and their selfishness end up being brought to life. Imagine your little broken story can become part of a larger story that ends well.[1]

—JOHN ORTBERG

SHE SEES BEYOND HERSELF

Living a life invested in the things of Jesus means we are *what-if* people. Courageous Girls are able to be confident in God because they have gradually learned He is in control and has a greater vision for His people. Though we are the apple of God's eye, we are not the center of the greatest story ever told. *He* is. When we begin to see the world through the heart of God, we are humbled by the gift to be used in His greater plan.

I have a list of quotes in the front of my Bible. C. S. Lewis's words are written at the top: "I believe in Christianity as I believe that the sun has risen: not only because I see it, but because by it I see everything else." Everything in life is clearer when we encounter Jesus and the light of His grace. Darkness dims when we can see by His light, even becoming the light in a world desperate to see hope in the flesh. John

1:5 says, "The light shines in the darkness, and the darkness has not overcome it." This light is Jesus.

Being in relationship with God, who is full of grace and mercy, reminds us that we are right where we are supposed to be. He has created us for such a time as this and will equip us with the resources needed to attune to those for whom His heart beats. Wherever we are in life, He still moves in and through us. Despite us, He does His thing. We may think in terms of "if only…, then…" (when I get more money, when my kids are older, or when my marriage is better). The list is endless. Yet, in God's economy, He does not need anything outside of Himself to make something out of nothing. God spoke, and the world was created out of empty darkness. Now that is power!

When we choose to follow Christ, that same Spirit of God is in us. We are literally in courage. God is the most courageous being, and He is in us. He wants to do something in you and then through you. There is a sign in our guest bathroom that I read almost every day. It says, "If you could not fail, what would you do?" You are experiencing the fruit of that message as you read this book! I am not extraordinary. I do, however, believe in an extraordinary God who *loves* to work in and through His people. All He wants is our yes, and He clearly respects our no.

It is so easy to get caught in the here-and-now rat race of life: focusing on the laundry, the meals, the dishes, the errands, the sports, the homework, and the laundry (yes, laundry is listed twice on purpose). Before we know it, the week is over and the haze of business has sucked up all our energy. Can I hear an amen? In the book *Screwtape Letters,* C. S. Lewis writes that the greatest tactic of the enemy is to keep Christians busy. It's not a creative strategy, but it's surely effective.[2]

It takes incredible discipline to stop and listen. Listen to what our deepest invitation is from our Creator. This is what a quiet time can help us do: see beyond the ordinary of life and lift our heads up to a greater destiny, one that is ordained by the King of the universe. There are seasons in life when we must embrace the daily tasks. There are other seasons when we must receive from others in order to heal, find comfort, and later offer that comfort to others. These are called seasons for a reason. None of us, even moms, are meant to live in the day-to-day tasks of life unless we know without a shadow of a doubt it is where God has asked us to be. There is no place I would rather be than in the pocket of His plan, and that can look different for each of His children. If you are a mom of several children, you can understand the delight and encouragement for each child's unique strengths.

Andy Crouch challenges "safe Christianity" when he says that "all flourishing requires risk."[3] This is not the kind of risk we take when we choose not to wear a seatbelt driving around town. He means the kind of risk that requires us to take time out of our safe community and engage in an impoverished one or traveling to where we could get ill. I'm talking about the kind of risk where Jesus touches a leper who is considered outcast, unclean, and contagious or spends a moment with the children despite their lack of value to adults in their culture. It might mean a great marriage. It might mean living with simplicity. It might mean serving our community without any expectations in return. I cannot tell you what it means for you and your daughter, but what I can tell you is that we are not to live inside a box, in safety, and expect to feel fulfilled or alive. That was not the design.

In his book *Culture Making: Recovering Our Creative Calling*, Crouch says, "The bigger the change we hope for, the longer we must be willing to invest, work for, and wait for it...I wonder what we Christians are known for in the world outside our churches. Are we known as critics, consumers, copiers, condemners of culture? I'm afraid so. Why aren't we known as cultivators—people who tend and nourish what is best in human culture, who do the hard and painstaking work to preserve the best of what people before us have done? Why aren't we known as creators—people who dare to think and do something that has never been thought or done before, something that makes the world more welcoming and thrilling and beautiful?...So do you want to make culture? Find a community, a small group who can lovingly fuel your dreams and puncture your illusions. Find friends and form a family who are willing to see grace at work in one another's lives, who can discern together which gifts and which crosses each has been called to bear. Find people who have a holy respect for power and a holy willingness to spend their power alongside the powerless. Find some partners in the wild and wonderful world beyond church doors. And then, together, make something of the world."[4] This is risk. This is obedience. This is Kingdom living. This is Courageous Girls.

SHE TRUSTS AND OBEYS

The word "obey," like the word "sin," has a really bad reputation in today's culture. Unfortunately, the word can be misconstrued and used to spiritually abuse people. But I want to make sure we consider the beauty and power in this word. Before I go any further, pause and consider the connotations you have with the word "obey." Is it good? Is it bad? Does it make you want to close the book or skip this chapter? Me too. I am a bit stubborn and need to find my own way. So obey feels stifling, restricting, and even claustrophobic to me. Or, it did before my epiphany that obedience is one of the roots to living fully.

I am a rule follower, *for the most part*. My dad taught me, "Rules are for people who cannot make good decisions. When you cannot make a good decision, refer to the rule." That principle has surely given me pause in blindly following rules and checking in with the Holy Spirit for a good decision. My desire to want to do the right thing comes out of a sense of not wanting to disappoint or cause trouble. That is the people pleaser in me. But God keeps putting me in situations where I feel like I have to disappoint people in order to follow Him. It's really frustrating and yet life altering at the same time. Even for a rule follower, obeying God is really hard for any human. Just because I want to do the "right thing" does not mean it's the "God thing," because it might not be what He is asking of me. Jesus was not exactly a rule follower. In fact, He bucked the system of His day in order to fulfill His mission. The Pharisees were not His fans, to say the least.

God has taught me how to move from being a people pleaser to a women of great faith, who obeys a God with a pretty remarkable plan. Three years ago, at our mama retreat in Central Oregon, we read the passage when Peter steps out of the boat. I asked every woman to consider one way God was calling her to step out and to keep her eyes on Jesus and not her circumstance. It was powerful to listen to the different ways God was asking us to trust Him — not in foolish ways, but in ways that required faith. That vulnerable moment of sharing with my CG mamas started something in me. Each of our examples were very diverse, unique to our own place in life, but completely right for each of our stories.

When we are caught between fear and insecurity, life is pretty small. Risk taking and acting on what we sense God leading us to do feels more like bondage than abundant life. About eight years ago, I was given the word *surrender* during a contemplative prayer retreat. It came just after Jeff and I launched our consulting and counseling business, Living Wholehearted. I did not know exactly what the word meant, but God would not let me move from that word for five years! Every year, I would ask for another word with great anticipation, but I would sense I was not done with *surrender*. What does that say about me? Am I really that slow? Or did God know what He was doing? Hindsight is really 20/20, and now I suspect He knew what He was doing.

In that five year process, God was challenging my people pleasing tendencies and forcing me to exercise my "no" muscle. I have helped many others with boundaries over the years and have recommended Lisa Terkeurst's book, "My Best Yes," too many times to count.[5] However, God was calling me to deeper waters. To surrender one's will over to God's will is one of the most risk taking experiences in which a person can engage. And yet, as a follower of Jesus, I think it's one of the most life altering and satisfying places I have ever been. On the front of my prayer journal years ago, I painted the word *surrender* with a tree trunk and the lyrics, "Bending beneath the weight of his wind and His mercy." *Oh how He loves us!*[6] Dreaming big and seeing those dreams come to fruition is one of my greatest desires for every Courageous

Mama and Girl. I'm not talking about just any dream, but one birthed from the sacred spaces of intimacy with the God who loves and knows us like no other. That is fully living.

God finally gave me a new word...well, two words actually: *trust* and *obey*. When those words came, I was a little nervous because I knew that He was asking me to start taking intentional risks. *Thanks, Andy Crouch.* I knew that the risks could not determine the outcome and that I would have to walk out on water without floating devices or safety nets. Only He could protect me, and only He could take care of the consequences. Our job is to trust Him and commit our way to Him. He does the rest. When obeying comes from a relationship rooted in love and grace, it really can feel like a no-brainer. And then, at other times...not so much. Sometimes, trust requires the kind of leaning into God that makes us feel like we are learning to swim all over again—like the moment when the swim instructor asks us to float, trusting that the water will not swallow us alive. If you have ever had a swim lesson with your kid, you understand the fear that instruction can create. It's challenging to lie back in the water without any reservations! However, once you do it, you are hooked. Psalm 37:3-7a says, "Trust in the Lord and do good. Dwell in the land and cultivate faithfulness. Delight yourself in the Lord and He will give you the desires of your heart. Commit your ways to the Lord, trust also in Him and He will do it. He will bring forth your righteousness as the light and your judgment as the noonday. Rest in the Lord and wait patiently on Him." There is so much richness in these verses, but the key here is to note the ebb and flow between our part and His. We trust in Him, delighting and committing our ways to Him, and let Him do the rest.

SHE ACCEPTS HER STARTING PLACE

Maybe dreaming comes naturally to you, or perhaps you tend to pop your own bubbles by unintentionally sabotaging or procrastinating your dreams. Maybe dreaming feels impractical and irresponsible. Maybe, in your mind, dreaming is only for other women, whatever that means to you. In so many of our cases, trauma and abuse have destroyed our ability to dream. In some instances, staying in our trauma paradigm—where our fears keep us stuck—feels safe, and so we become highly conservative and controlling, and only venture into known waters. Fear of the unknown becomes the marker of our life. In other cases, we become irrational, impulsive, and only do what will take the pain immediately away. The natural consequences of abuse and trauma snatch our hope of tomorrow and cause us to prepare ceaselessly for the worst-case scenario. Trust and obedience seem too scary for someone who was deeply harmed, violated, or betrayed by someone they trusted.

I want you to know that our God is not abusive and will never violate our will. He designed us for so much and will allow us to take as long as we need to heal. He is compassionate and patient. There is grace for where we are today, and He will help us take one step at a time toward dreaming. Healing requires new thinking, new experiences, and new practices that repair our neuropathways in order for our body and "gut" to catch up to. It will take time. For those who are unable to dream yet, we can walk alongside them as hope agents. Trauma can be healed, and the shame that paralyzes us can be lifted, but it requires time and consistent safe places to land before we can dream big. We all need to know someone can catch us when we fall. The step to get help and heal is an intentional risk. It could be your first!

There is grace for where you are, and I hope this chapter paints a picture of what could be for you and your daughter. Healing from our past is an essential ingredient to dreaming big. It requires one action step at a time in the present in order to impact the future and bring hope for tomorrow. Trust and obedience are the other ingredients. Just like our daughters, we must know that our Father in heaven is good, kind, and loves us before we will obey. Obeying out of fear, obligation, or because we think He is angry or critical, produces nothing more than performance.

In King David's confessional, Psalm 51:17, he says, "For You do not delight in sacrifice, otherwise I would give it; You are not pleased with burnt offering. The sacrifices of God are a broken spirit; A broken and a contrite heart, O God, You will not despise." God wants a complete heart, not our sacrifices. Obedience without a heart smells fishy to God, and, let's be honest, even to others. Sometimes we think we can fool people, but most can tell the difference between someone being authentic in their "good works" and someone who is just trying really hard. When we are able to heal, we can see that God is not abusive but only good. Obeying out of desire and a trusting relationship with God is the greatest risk of all and leads to quite an adventure. Missionaries are not the only ones who have a call on their lives. Moms all over the world are change agents in their sphere of influence.

Have you considered God's vision for you and your life? Does it move beyond your next vacation or even the next soccer game? Maybe you are just trying to make ends meet or find time to sleep. I hear you, and I am not trying to add more to your plate. I just want you to know that God is at work in and through you, and this life is meant for so much more than you or I can imagine.

There is grace for where you are, and you are right where you are supposed to be. Start here; start now. Ask God to show you the next step. When you do not know anything else to do, start with reading God's Word. Psalm 119:105 says, "Your word is a lamp for my feet, a light on my path." Start with where you are. Then He will part the waters, and He will show you the way.

SHE REFLECTS HIS LOVE TO OTHERS

Obedience means people will know we belong to God. "By this we know that we love the children of God, when we love God and obey his commandments. For this is the love of God, that we keep his commandments. And his commandments are not burdensome" (1 John 5:2-3). His Word tells us how to live, but even more, His Spirit invites us into a personal journey with Him. Dreaming and allowing God to lead the way lead to a thrilling life.

God is not a genie who grants our every wish. However, *if* God is orchestrating His dream through us, it will happen. It surely does not happen in the manner in which we think it will, and it will likely take some time and intention on our part. God's way often has side roads, off roads, and some apparent dead ends. The first way we know our dream is aligned with God is through a grid of scripture. God does not tell us anything contrary to what He has already declared in the Bible. So when someone tells me that God "said" to divorce his wife for another woman, we can refer to God's Word for clarification (scripture makes clear God would not tell us to do that). Second, God asks us to do things that bring us peace. That does not mean we will not have moments when we feel scared or nervous, but it does mean that deep down we have confident peace. If you have lived your whole life pleasing people and doing what is expected of you, then you might need slow and steady practice here. Usually, seeking the counsel of another person can help us discern if our leaning is from God, hormones or something we ate. Finally, if it's God's direction or call, He will make it happen. It sounds too simple, but it is biblically true.

Finally, as we discern our dreams with God, remember that His ways do not always align with our timeline. Noah waited 120 years before the boat he was building in faith would actually save his family's lives from the "laughable" rains that he claimed would flood the earth. Moses was in the desert for forty years before he was called to lead the Israelites out of Egypt. Jesus didn't start His ministry until He was 30. We do not have to strive to make His dreams in us come alive; our job is simply to trust and obey.

Let God do what He is good at—using ordinary people to do extraordinary things. There is nothing He cannot do. So allow yourself to dream. Then, allow your daughter(s) to dream. Allow her to think beyond today, and then step back and imagine what she would need to pray, do, or ask of God to take a step toward that dream. It's not the dreaming that is most important, but the relationship required with God and the building up of our faith. Let's empower our daughters to dream and then be blown away by how they partner with God to participate in a greater cause.

SHE ACCEPTS SHE IS NEITHER PERFECT NOR BORING (THE TWO GO HAND IN HAND)

God uses humanity even when we continually make mistakes. Dreaming beyond our abilities leaves room for God's mighty power to move through our frailness. Brené Brown says, "Understanding the difference between healthy striving and perfectionism is critical to laying down the shield and picking up your life. Research shows that perfectionism hampers success. In fact, it's often the path to depression, anxiety, addiction, and life paralysis."[7] Amen, sister! Perfectionism kills the mind, body, and soul of so many moms and daughters. Let's learn to embrace the messiness of a house, the awkward blunders of our children in public, the far-too-real moments in our marriages, and the many times we fumble over ourselves. Perfection is boring. Every risk taker knows that failing is a part of the greater journey to success. So let's quit trying. Malcolm Gladwell shares his research on a history of misfits, underdogs, and little guys.[8] He tells how our limitations might be the very thing that develops strength within us for a greater cause. For example, having dyslexia can develop other skill sets and attune our ability to navigate uncharted terrain. What we see as a "mistake" or "imperfection," God sees as an opportunity and grows another muscle to be used on purpose.

Let go of the need to please others. Let go of the need to post on social media. Let go of the need to look a certain way. Let go of knowing how it will all work out. Dreaming requires the ability to move forward even when the finished product is not fully in place. I get that it's easier said than done for most, but for those who need to practice the gift of being human, it's important to start by "failing." Start small: let your daughter go to school in an outfit that does not match, or cancel a commitment without lying about why. Instead, truthfully admit you need a break and overcommitted yourself. Start by not wearing makeup when you go to the store. Start by not showering and playing with your daughter instead. (Oh wait, that one might happen already if you have littles in the home!)

In any case, Brown reminds us, "To love someone fiercely, to believe in something with your whole heart, to celebrate a fleeting moment in time, to fully engage in a life that doesn't come with guarantees—these are risks that involve vulnerability and often pain. But, I'm learning that recognizing and leaning into the discomfort of vulnerability teaches us how to live with joy, gratitude and grace." On the other hand, "Perfectionism is a self-destructive and addictive belief system that fuels this primary thought: If I look perfect, and do everything perfectly, I can avoid or minimize the painful feelings of shame, judgment, and blame."[9]

We have already established that pain is essential in the human experience, and we cannot feel the thrill of a full life without the despair of the valleys. You cannot turn off the negative emotions without turning off the positive ones too. So, in dreaming big, we have the grand invitation to participate in a far greater purpose than our comfort and success. Meeting our own needs, though God cares for those dearly, should not be our end goal. He is up to something far more grand, and He asks you, me and our daughters to walk with Him so that He can show us what that is. Like Lucy in *The Lion, the Witch and the Wardrobe*, we have to be willing to step through a door. We do not always know where that door will lead, but we do know that Aslan is always present in the process. Others may question our faith, like Peter and Susan. Some might even try to sabotage it, like Edmond. And then there will be some who are like the Professor, who see beyond the ordinary with us. Regardless, being a dreamer can lead others to healing, hope, and redemption in ways they could never see themselves.

Courageous Girls dream big and allow God to use them for His glory, whether we see the whole picture or not. We know it's really not about us or about producing anything. It's about a relationship in which God loves us so much that He wants to partner with us to reach the world one person at a time. Joining forces with a community of moms and daughters can help us have more courage, encouraging one another to move beyond the mundane darkness of life. I have personally watched every single mom in our CG group step into her dreams and find joy. Being a mom is one of the greatest callings in life, but we are not defined by the title. We are defined by our position with Christ. Therefore, our dreams are not our own. They are planted in us and grown through us, by faith in a God who is ever constant, compassionate, and sees the greater needs in our world. Courage sees beyond our kitchen sink and says yes to God's call. Trust and obey with me. The world needs a few more women stepping out of the boat and keeping our eyes on Jesus.

Takeaway

Write five things you would *love* to do if there were no time constraints, money issues, or other responsibilities in your life. Write down five barriers that keep you from accomplishing those five dreams. Note that these are not necessarily the dreams God has for you, but it's a starting point to assess where you currently are in life and to see how God shapes your vision. Then read and pray Psalm 37:3-7 over yourself and your daughter. It says, *trust* in the Lord...*delight* in the Lord...*commit* your ways...*He will* bring forth...*Rest* in the Lord and *wait* patiently on Him. Notice which word or phrase stands out to you the most. Then ask God to show you an action step related to that word or phrase He is asking you to step into.

Take It a Step Further

Memorize Ephesians 3:16-21 with your daughter. This is the founding verse behind Courageous Girls. Keep a journal to watch and see how God uses these words to move in your life and the life of your daughter.

10

She Practices Rhythms of Rest

Most of us are more tired than we know at the soul level. We are teetering on the brink of dangerous exhaustion, and we cannot do anything else until we have gotten some rest...we can't really engage [any spiritual disciplines] until solitude becomes a place of rest for us rather than another place for human striving and hard work.[1]

— RUTH HALEY BARTON

Not all of us can do great things. But we can do small things with great love.

- MOTHER TERESA

SHE EMBRACES THE MINISTRY OF PRESENCE

The gift of time and being fully present are rare these days. Sometimes, all we long for as moms or daughters, is just to *be*—to be together with no agenda, no demands, no lectures and no expectations. In fact, *being present* is one of the three essential ingredients for a thriving relationship, both vertically and horizontally. As I mentioned in a previous chapter, the other two ingredients include *I have a voice* and *you have a voice*. Though it sounds so simple, the ability to be fully present is an advanced discipline and does not come easy to many. Most of the CG curriculum is helping moms and daughters to discover and practice these components of healthy relationship.

Being present not only requires us to engage our bodies, minds and spirits, but it also requires that we let go of the past and the worries of tomorrow. Whew! That sounds like a tall order in Western culture in light of all the other concerns we've considered in this book. Niequist is right when she says, "The world will tell you how to live, if you let it. Don't let it. Take up your space. Raise your voice. Sing your song. This is your chance to make or remake a life that thrills you." She goes on to say, "*Present* means we understand that the here and now is sacred, sacramental, threaded through with divinity even in its plainness. Especially in its plainness."[2] Tomorrow is not a guarantee, friend. And the more sober-minded we are, the more we know this to be true.

My husband, Jeff, was almost killed in a car accident his senior year of high school. This life-altering experience taught Jeff two things. First, God is the main reason we are here. Second, all that is important is the present and the relationships in the current season. I have received from a man who knows that tomorrow can be taken away at the drop of a hat. He lives more fully present than most. You and I both know that life has a way of bringing many surprises. Recognizing that this moment might be the only we have helps us reframe any situation.

I remember a moment many years ago sitting on my couch; my living room was a mess, my kids were running around singing and dancing, and there was a pile of laundry about the size of Mount Everest next to me. In that moment, I took a deep breath and could sense the Holy Spirit reminding me to just be present. I smelled the fresh laundry, listened to the piano as my youngest banged away on its keys, and watched my oldest (at the time only 5) twirl in circles in her little ballet tutu. The mess around me reminded me there was life. Life *abundant*. There was nothing profound or out of the ordinary, but something struck me deep in my soul with a whisper I have not forgotten—*this is life, and it's good.*

A Courageous Girl is firmly rooted in gratitude and in the ability to be fully present and fully alive, while holding tightly to Jesus in the midst of whatever is occurring around her. In order to have this perspective, we need regular rhythms in the Word, we need to check in with our souls, and we need to hear from the Lord. As Ecclesiastes reminds us, there is a time for everything. Tuning in to what is needed *here and now* is often the challenge. Let's explore the variety of ways we can practice rhythms of rest so that our daughters will be able to see the ebbs and flows of a healthy life in all its glorious "plainness."

SHE ACCEPTS THE INVITATION TO REST

Opportunity has become an ever present idol in the lives of our daughters. The cultural norm to make sure our kids do not miss out on anything: the best schooling, tutoring, music teachers, sports, camps, birthday parties and more is overwhelming. Moms are notorious for being the caretakers of the community; they are often the first to get up and the last to go to bed. Sometimes we can confuse rest for laziness or even selfishness. Add a little Jesus in the mix, and we can feel convicted by false guilt to do more, be more, and fill our days with good things. Learning to slow down, spending time in quiet and solitude is truly a discipline for many of us moms who carry the weight of our worlds to discern His voice in the midst of all the noise. In the midst of the noise around us — social media, news, work, school, coaches, church, marriages, kids, bills, and our own minds — times of solitude and self-care may sound like a luxury for most moms. However, for true transformation in our lives and in the lives of our daughters, rest is a necessity for those who want sustained health in their souls, relationships, and mothering.

We can model to our girls that life has rhythms: there's a time for work and a time for rest, a time for serving and a time for receiving, a time to be serious and a time to play. Modeling rest will not only help our girls be rooted in the gospel of grace, it will help them live a sustainable life on the foundation of Christ. The messages that say, "it's all up to me," or "I need to be responsible," or "no one will step up to the plate," can actually be detrimental to our spiritual journey and and create a lopsided way of living. Striving and always taking care of everyone and everything around us can zap joy and introduce all kinds of issues into our lives, such as codependency, selfishness, narcissism, bitterness, adrenal fatigue, burn out, health problems like

IBS or headaches, anxiety and depression. I cannot tell you how many women I hear say, "I want someone to take care of me for once!" If our daughters never see us take time out for ourselves, with our God, and for our own good, our daughters will notice. Jesus said, "Love others as you love yourself." If you do a poor job of loving yourself, the logic leads us to believe you are doing a poor job of loving others. Ouch! One of my dear mentors reminded me that if your love for yourself is based on all you can accomplish and all you contribute to the world around you, then your expectations and love for others will also be based on what they can give you rather than on loving them as God's creation. Until we can understand how to love ourselves and others simply because they exist, we will not be able to love others well.

Even Jesus, the God of the universe in the flesh, took time away from the crowds to be in solitude and relationship with His Father. Even Jesus needed to quiet the noise and be present with His heavenly Parent. Mark 1:34-38 says, "And He healed many who were ill with various diseases, and cast out many demons; and He was not permitting the demons to speak, because they knew who He was. In the early morning, while it was still dark, Jesus got up, left the house, and went away to a secluded place, and was praying there. Simon and his companions searched for Him; they found Him, and said to Him, 'Everyone is looking for You'" (NIV). So, when you sit down on the couch for a moment of peace to stare out the window and observe the beauty around you, and your children immediately interrupt you, remember that you are in good company! Simon and all his companions searched for Jesus when He tried to be alone. So real, right? The truth is that being alone may not always work out, but nonetheless we must recognize that it is essential to being a healthy Courageous Mom. We must learn to model rest, and not the more common model of lopsided living (serve, do, give, do, crash).

SHE STAYS FOCUSED

What always strikes me about the Mark passage is the way that Jesus clearly knows where to go and what to do after He spends time with the Father. Jesus received direction in the quiet places, in prayer through exploring the sacred parts of the soul with His Father. At this time, many people had heard of Jesus' ability to heal, cast out demons, and preach good news. People were following Him (everywhere!), and despite their requests in this passage, the most compassionate, loving, and merciful God in the flesh said, "Let us go somewhere else so that I can do what I came for." I can imagine that those people might have felt rejected, frustrated, or even angry. But in Jesus' mind, He was focused on His Father's business, not the people's agenda.

The pressure to say yes to the immediate and urgent needs before us keeps us from abundant life. Spending time checking in with our own soul, asking God to search us and tell us what He knows, confessing and aligning ourselves with Him, and listening for His voice happen when we pull away from the needs before us and allow ourselves to be still. A couple times a year, we invite women out to the Living Wholehearted Lodge & Retreat for a day of contemplative prayer. This day of silence has become some of the most treasured and anticipated days because women need help slowing down. The CG website has ideas for day or weekend retreats, along with a guide for more contemplative getaways.

SHE GOES TO JESUS TO FIND REST

I have meditated on Matthew 11:28-29 for years to remind my soul to go to the One who quenches my deepest thirst. The Message translation says that Jesus asks His disciples, "Are you tired? Worn out? Burned out on religion? Come to me. Get away with me and you'll recover your life. I'll show you how to take a real rest. Walk with me and work with me—watch how I do it. Learn the unforced rhythms of grace. I won't lay anything heavy or ill-fitting on you. Keep company with me and you'll learn to live freely and lightly." Jesus was speaking to the Israelites who were burdened with a legalistic system and a long to-do list from the Pharisees. Their cultural expectations left them with guilt, frustration, and disappointment. Jesus offers us something completely apart from religiosity and the pressure to measure up to perfect standards. His grace invites us to enter rest. Rest is one of the most amazing aspects of a relationship with Christ, because it means more than just sleeping. It is the kind of rest that means "It is well with my soul."

The most profound idea of rest is found in Hebrews 3:7–4:11. God had worked and created for six days when He spoke the world into existence. God did not get tired, but He chose to lay down His work and call it good. I love that He did not call His work amazing, excellent, or even perfect. He called it *good*. Our attempts to innovate and improve are not for God's glory but for our own glory. That is such a humbling concept because God chose to rest and then offered us the gift to rest on Sabbath. It's unfortunate that most of us will not receive the gift because we have "too much" to do.

Just like most idols, coveting our time can take the place of a relationship with God. Productivity and doing things for Jesus can become more of a focus for us than Jesus Himself. Martha knows what this is like as she slaves away in the kitchen while her sister, Mary, sits at the feet of Jesus. The dialogue between Martha and Jesus is fascinating: "Lord, don't you care that my sister has left me to do the work by myself? Tell her to help me!" "Martha, Martha," the Lord answered, "you are worried and upset about many things, but few things are needed—or indeed only one. Mary has chosen what is better, and it will not be taken away from her" (Luke 10:38-42, NIV).

What is better? It is time with Jesus. It's not doing *for* Jesus, but instead learning to be still and know that He is God. Martha was worrying about things that did not ultimately matter. It is important to help our children with homework and to give them opportunities to explore their talents, experiences, and minds. However, when all is said and done, the Millennial and Now generations are the most talented than any other generation. Many of them started businesses by the time they were thirteen and have more degrees than generations prior. Yet, I am not sure they hold the record for being the most fulfilled. The soul that finds security in a relationship with Christ will be able to set boundaries, say no, take a Sabbath, and have a regular quiet time.

These are not legalistic tasks to accomplish but instead are practical ways to model to our children that life is not all about what we do but about who we do it with and why.

SHE STAYS IN TUNE WITH HER BODY

Another practical way we can find rest is by staying in tune with our bodies. As we learn that our bodies give us insight to what we need and how we feel, we do a better job of recognizing the rhythms we need to stay ahead of the curve. Often sickness, fatigue, moodiness, anxiety, depression, and physical problems can be symptoms of stress and lack of rest, maybe even unresolved hurts. A good question to ask yourself is, "What do I feel in my body right now?" If you do not sincerely know, then start by asking God to tell you. If you still do not know, you may be either numb or fully dissociated from your body. You have learned to live only in your "thinking brain" to avoid feeling; it is time to learn what is happening below the neck.

Many dysfunctional ways of living are birthed out of a disconnection from our bodies. We need to learn how to pay attention to our physical cues. Giving name to the level of intensity we feel in our bodies, even applying a scale from 1 to 10, will help us measure what our bodies need in the moment and keep us connected. When we pay attention to our bodies, similar to a clumsy person in a Chihuly glass museum who has to consciously think about where they walk and the pace at which they move (I might relate!), peace is possible regardless of circumstance. When we ignore our bodies, we can guarantee something is going to break. Learning to tune in to our bodies and identify the level of intensity we are feeling in a particular area help us prevent a flight, fight, or freeze response. It also prevents us from "flipping our lids," as Dr. Siegel suggests.[3] When our lids flip, we can guarantee that we are running only on fumes and that our body is experiencing copious amounts of stress hormones. The effects on us and those around us will eventually take their toll.

I am notorious for ignoring the dashboard in my car, and I have way too many stories to tell where the ending was not so happy. Lesson learned: pay attention to the warning signs on the dashboard! The lifestyle of forging ahead when we are overworked, tired and stressed should initiate internal sirens that tell us it's time to shift to a lower gear, or maybe even hit the brakes. When our bodies are trying to function at a high level of intensity, it's like our body's engine is catching on fire. The emotions we feel in our bodies (anxiety, anger, guilt, shame, grief, fear, etc.) can help us cue into when it's time to pause, evaluate our needs, and find rest in the Lord. Sometimes our bodies communicate before our hearts, minds and souls. Helping our daughters learn to regulate their own emotions and body intensity is one of the key lessons in the CG curriculum. However, in order for them to be able to regulate, we have to learn it first so that they can see it in action. Courageous Girls learn how to do this—not perfectly, but well. My hope is that this type of mind-body awareness will be both yours and your daughter's "normal" before she reaches adulthood.

If you need help to find simple ways to rest and even schedule it into your day, here are some ideas:

1. Take a quiet time in the morning or evening.
2. Schedule a walk between meetings.
3. Take deep breaths to trick your brain into believing you are calm.
4. Schedule a half-day prayer retreat in a quiet location.
5. Go on a mini spa vacation in the bathtub or take a longer shower.
6. Revel in your five senses (smell, touch, feel, see, and hear) and enjoy the moment.
7. Exercise and allow your body to shift hormonally.
8. Try journaling (research truly backs this one up).
9. Stop multitasking and do one thing at a time at a slower pace.
10. Put on music and allow the words and the rhythm to calm your brain.

Three ways we can stay in tune with our bodies are through exercising, eating well, and drinking water. So often we forget that self-care includes the basics, like going to the restroom when our body is actually cuing us to go. In all seriousness, this can be the most basic practice for moms and daughters. Just go to the bathroom! Life will continue if you take two minutes to excuse yourself. Drinking water and listening to hunger cues are other ways to grow in the rhythms of rest. This teaches our girls that being healthy is not about how we look but how we feel. When food becomes the coping mechanism as either a way to control or numb life with quick fixes, we have misplaced its purpose. I have never been a fan of diets, mostly because I love all foods. However, I *am* a fan of listening to what our bodies need and crave. If you truly pay attention, you will be surprised to find that your body will tell you what it needs. The next time you go to the refrigerator or pantry, pause long enough to first see if you are hungry (and not bored, angry, sad, or lonely). Then, check in with your tummy to see what sounds good. Protein? Dairy? Chocolate? Allowing food to be a fuel and not a "good or evil" will prevent our daughters from framing food as the enemy. In fact, food is a pleasure and a gift from the Lord. When it's in its rightful place, our bodies will naturally adjust the "right size" for our own frame and God's design. Trying to be someone else's body shape is playing into the comparison game.

Finding rest in our body size, and in the food we consume, is truly half of the battle. The final half of the battle is seeing movement and exercise as a way to process our emotions, clean out our organs, receive feel-good hormones, and maintain a sustainable body weight that helps us do good things with God. This is a process, and throughout many years of walking with women of every shape and size *and* being a woman of different shapes and sizes throughout many seasons, the greatest "diet" I have found is simply staying in tune with one's emotional health and what the body requests. Occasionally, I do crave a kale or spinach salad. I also crave burgers and fries. Since giving up dairy due to an intolerance in my digestive system, I rarely crave ice cream anymore. When we truly listen to what makes us feel good, we will find that our bodies adjust. Most of our body weight is related more to genes and emotional baggage. Yes, what we eat and how we exercise do impact our body size, but when those are the main focus, we will always find ourselves relapsing. Finding rest in whatever size we are and tuning in to the deeper needs of the soul and body will produce lasting change.

SHE CAN BE "BORED" AND "UNPLUG"

No matter what the day entails, we can encourage our daughter to take 20-30 minutes a day to be by herself and engage in something she wants to do. Maybe that means reading, playing legos, dancing, or playing with a pet. Do not get so fixated on a need to read the Bible or journal; though, as she gets older, this rhythm is important to navigate. When our girls are younger, we might engage in quiet time with them in the mornings or evenings, depending on our routines and lifestyle. In any case, the point is to integrate a way of being alone, without a device or performing a scheduled activity or chore, so that we can cultivate meaningful rest.

Sometimes our daughters might say they are bored when we create this kind of routine in our homes. Resist the temptation to rescue them from their struggle. Dr. Kevin Lehman, a well-known psychologist and author in Christian circles, says that we need to let our children be bored like we need to feed them.[4] Tongue in cheek, he reminds us we are raising kids, not gerbils, so we need to get off the hamster wheel that perpetuates stressed-out homes. The Millennials (born 1983-2000) were the first generation in history to have a scheduled childhood, and the phenomenon has only become increasingly intense for their children, the "Nows." Whether you identify with the Millennials or Gen X, your way of doing life impacts whether or not your daughter sees a value in giving and receiving in life.

Learning how to be bored, with no agenda or entertainment, is a fundamental life skill. A lack of ability to sit still, rest, find joy in the ordinary, or cultivate creativity without clear direction directly links to addictions, rigid thinking, and interference with intimate relationships. Not everything in our lives needs to be scheduled, entertaining, or productive. We are human "beings," not human "doings." Let's teach our daughters to be present by learning to be more so ourselves. Try pausing during the day to hug her for more than thirty seconds *just because*. Practice sitting still, or go for a walk and notice how creation reveals the nature of God.

Finally, take a moment and access the level of involvement you have with your phone and other digital devices. If we are honest, most of us are addicted and compulsively look to see what else is happening outside this very moment. Part of that problem has to do with a little pleasure hormone, dopamine, that activates every time we notice an incoming email, text, or call. The first rule of helping our daughters engage in a digital world is managing our own. Scheduling "on" and "off" times for ourselves, or taking longer to get back to someone via text, can slow down our Pavlov's Dog responses. It has been clinically proven that technology increases anxiety, activates stress hormones, and creates forms of ADD-like symptoms. Due to increased levels of sensory overload, moms and daughters alike have shorter fuses, less tolerance for interruption, and struggle to stand in line without looking at their phone. What happened to taking brief moments of inactivity to enjoy the smell of the air, take a deep breath, or look into our daughter's eyes? Another way we can manage our digital devices is engaging in downtime as a family, when everyone puts their devices in the same place and devotes the rest of the evening to family time. Not only will this calm everyone's brains, but your daughter might actually talk with you and engage with you more regularly.

SHE PROTECTS HER WHITE SPACE

"White space" is the white margin on the outside of any paper.[5] It's the boundary between where a person writes in the lines and where the writing stops. I am guilty of writing in the white space whenever I take notes. I like the creativity and efficiency of packing one side of a note page full of good insights, only flipping to the other side if necessary. The downside is that I also do this in my life. Packing every hour of my day with important and good things to do feels efficient. However, wisdom would say to leave the edge of the paper, and some space in my schedule, "just in case" life takes a quick turn. (And we all know it can and it does.) Jamming our lives full of activities does not reflect a life well lived. I often get the question "How do you do it all, Terra?" The truth is, I don't. I have learned the art of delegation in my business, ministry, Courageous Girls, and even with my children. I love to help others discover their gifts, talents, and contribution while we co-create together. It is not always efficient, but it surely is a helpful way to leave margin and see others experience their potential. Having our girls help around the house or help us get ready for a Courageous Girls meeting teaches them principles of shared responsibility, value for others, team work, and ownership.

I also have to practice "time blocking" by creating white space on my calendar. I have days and weekends with no scheduled plans, which allows me to be spontaneous and in the moment. No one else knows I am doing this apart from my family. Time blocking is similar to financial budgeting. Similar to how we save, give, and spend our moneys, we can also plan and delegate our time in a similar manner. Both are forms of resources. Try practicing having a couple nights a week with no sports, dinner dates, or church activities. It will leave room for relationship building. Maybe limit the number of activities for your daughter so that she can enjoy margin in her life. There is not a direct clinical correlation, but many anxieties and behavioral issues we see in our offices are partially due to the overworked, overtired, and relationship-deprived routines in a child's life. Children need margin just to be kids.

When we intentionally choose to leave white space in our routines, we find more moments when we can say yes to a spontaneous request from our daughter to play, read or spend time with her. Margin gives us freedom to say yes to watching a movie together or cuddling a little longer at bedtime. As women, we know what it is like to make a spontaneous request to our husbands or friends. When they accept our offer to spend time together, it deposits something valuable into our love tanks. White space also gives us breathing room when emergencies happen. No one plans for these, but leaving time between the larger tasks in our days, weeks, and months can be our saving grace. It seems a little ironic that we need to schedule boredom, time for spontaneity, or unexpected emergencies, but, in many cases, it might be the only way we find the "unscheduled" time.

SHE CARES FOR HERSELF AND PLAYS

Self-care comes in many forms and is unique to you. My self-care involves gardening, walking with friends, exercising, and journaling. What does your self-care look like? Can your daughter see you participating in self-care? Does she even know it exists? Are you modeling it to her in tangible ways and allowing her to have her own time for herself, away from siblings, family, and other demands of school or activities? Let her be the motivation for you to start caring for yourself. Otherwise, you are teaching your daughter how to be a care-taker at the expense of her own needs. Co-dependency is a label for those of us who live to make everyone else happy at the cost of our own health. Love is not co-dependent.

A destructive belief that I often hear around this topic is that "it's selfish to love myself." But Jesus said to love others as you love yourself. God's Word beautifully illustrates a give-and-take relationship between the "I" and "other." Grace is at the center of that tension. I love the moments when Jesus receives from others in the scriptures. When Jesus initially entered into His ministry, He spent forty days in the wilderness where He fasted and was tempted by the enemy. Jesus resisted and it says the devil fled. And then, "angels came and attended to Jesus" (see Matthew 4:11). We all know and think of Jesus as a giver, but He also received. Every Christmas we are reminded that the God of the universe came down from the heavens and became a baby. For many years, Jesus was cared for and nurtured by Mary and Joseph. Learning how to receive is a powerful way for us to remember our humanity. And recognizing our humanity keeps us connected to the foundation of our faith—we have needs that can only be met by receiving. A few core needs include security, acceptance, significance and hope. We also need to be known, seen, and loved. Self-care is a kinesthetic discipline. Even sleeping when tired will bear much fruit. Keeping the rhythm of give-and-take through our own self-care and meeting the needs of others help us live in the tension of grace.

An all-or-nothing mindset can signal performance-based faith and hidden trauma. ("I have to perform in order to be loved.") Self-care is part of loving ourselves well. We can liken it to the oxygen mask in the airplane. If you have ever flown on a plane, you know that passengers are taught to put on their oxygen mask before assisting others, including our children. Similar to parenting, we must make sure we have fueled our own bodies, souls, and minds in order to be helpful to girls (and all the others who call on us). Self-care does not have to cost money. In fact, I would encourage you to keep it simple. The simpler it is, the more likely you will do it.

The CG curriculum addresses ways to move beyond our own comfort to serve another. In fact, we encourage moms and daughters to practice this regularly. We wash one another's feet, make dates to get our hair and nails done, and take turns lifting up other moms and daughters with words of encouragement and prayers. Try it yourself. Schedule regular times of getting away, sitting on the couch and staring out the window, taking a walk around the block, or curling up and reading a favorite book. Simply slowing down long enough to breathe in for four counts and slowly exhale for six counts can be life changing for many moms. There is no need to keep going, especially if your body is telling you it's reaching high intensity levels. These small ways of receiving invite us to participate in learning how to stay in the tension of loving others as we love ourselves or as God has loved us.

Part of self-care includes receiving care from others as well as learning how to play. Psychiatrist Stuart Brown, founder of the National Institute for Play in Carmel Valley, California, found that "Play is a basic human need as essential to our well-being as sleep, so when we're low on play, our minds and bodies notice."[6] Based on our Core Values Index and family-of-origin, some of us engage in play easily. Others of us need to have play demonstrated because our whole lives have been about work, responsibility, and production. "What all play has in common," Brown says, "is that it offers a sense of engagement and pleasure, takes the player out of a sense of time and place, and the experience of doing it is more important than the outcome." Sounds a little like grace to me—undeserved favor. We do not always have to earn time to play, but we do need time to play, laugh, engage with our daughters, enjoy our friendships, and create something simply for the sake of the art of creating. Play helps us recognize that life is about the process over the product and the effort rather than the outcome.

Play has been found to speed up learning, enhance productivity, and increase job satisfaction. Playing together in simple ways, like going to a concert, can enhance bonding and communication at home. Playful adults respond to stressors differently and seemingly with more ease. You might say that those who play have higher levels of resilience. Play-therapy expert Dr. Garry Landreth says that play is to children what talking is for adults.[7] Play is the language of our daughters, and it allows them to process life. After 9/11, researchers found children processing through their play, crashing planes into the block towers they built. Adults do not need to process in this way, and playing *all* the time is not the point. The point is, we should not dismiss the power of play, as it benefits you, your daughter, and your connection to God. Recall some of the things you enjoyed as a kid and allow yourself to try it again. Play hopscotch. Play dress-up with your daughter. Order off the kids menu and get a prize. What is holding you back from play? Take a moment to ponder your ability to play, and consider how you might try to today.

SHE EMBRACES THE ORDINARY MOMENTS

Over the years, as *American Idol, The Voice,* and *So You Think You Can Dance* have become our new realities, I have noticed that the temptation to sensationalize everything we do is hindering our joy and our contentment. We think we can or must go from being a stay-at-home mom to a YouTube sensation by recording everything we do and posting it for all to see. Personally, I do not want you to peep into my life. Privacy, solitude, and downtime have become more valuable than gold. I choose not to engage in social media because I know my tendency to compare myself to others and can recognize the urge to strive for something outside of my personal call from God. This is my own conviction, and there is no judgment on yours. But I do want you to know your limits. What helps you stay content in where God has placed you? What causes you to stir internally and externally?

In God's economy, extraordinary living can look a little old school, especially if we put the standard up against the world's standard. The heroes of our faith are the individuals who put one foot in front of the next and did *only* what God was asking of them in the moment. Mother Teresa is one of my heroes. She realized that by loving one person at a time, and helping them to die with dignity, she could change the world. Her desire to do something big was met in the simple love of caring for those right in front of her. She got it. She did not have a platform on social media, and yet the world heard about her over time as she was faithful in the small things.

> Whoever can be trusted with very little can also be trusted with much, and whoever is dishonest with very little will also be dishonest with much. (Luke 16:10, NIV)

Mother Teresa took this verse to heart. She once said, "Be faithful in small things, because it is in them that your strength lies." She also said, "We ourselves feel that what we are doing is just a drop in the ocean. But the ocean would be less because of that missing drop."[8] Our contributions matter to God, whether it's praying for someone, making them a meal, changing their diaper, or looking them in the eyes. We need to recognize that nothing is too small or too ordinary in God's kingdom. He sees you and values what you bring to Him. You are the contribution.

There are simple ways you can let your daughter know you value ordinary moments in life, such as letting her interrupt you occasionally when on a phone call or in the middle of a task. Pause from what you're doing and look her in the eyes. Let her know she is more important. Or if she asks for your attention, drop what you are doing and go to her. Sit with her and engage in her "ordinary" world when she invites you to be with her. Or take her for a walk with no other agenda but to spent time together. The ordinary monthly meetings where moms and daughters gather together to discuss, pray, read the Word, do a craft, and talk can be some of the moments when she feels your love the most. The regular drop of time, attention, and intentional love speak louder than our words. Maybe spend time every night just lying with her and letting her talk, perhaps by identifying a high and low from her day. These are things that are mentioned at memorials, on Mother's Day, and when our children leave the house when they are grown. At the end of our lives, these are the moments—not the accomplishments or accolades—we wish we could get back.

When I was an undergrad, I took a ministry course that helped us navigate our specific passions in life. I will never forget when I heard the professor declare, "Your life is your ministry." It blew my mind. *You mean being me is enough for God and His kingdom purposes?* I have unpacked that simple truth over the years, and I still stand firm upon it after twenty years. Having the courage to be myself allows me to minister to anyone before me. This seems too simple to be real, but it's the true message of grace. More than anything, God wants our whole heart. We can truly rest on that.

Courageous Mama, you are loved. You are seen. You have a purpose. You are invited into intimate relationships with God and others. You are allowed to make mistakes and they can be redeemed. You can rest and allow God to move. You are invited to partner with His power to do more than we can ask or imagine. It's time to awaken our senses and recognize the times. Do not be caught up in the whirlwind of panic or dismissal that is common to the world, but take hold of the power we have been given by our God. He is in us. He is around us. He has gone before us. He is behind us. And He is the One upon whom we stand—with confidence, resilience, and grace.

Our daughters are crying out for women to show them the way; they need us to lead. Imagine a generation of girls who know they are loved and love others well. Imagine a generation of girls who speak life and encouragement and hope into those around them. Imagine a generation of girls who not only stand up for their own value and worth but also for the value and worth of others. Imagine a generation of girls who lean into the mighty power of our God and live into their destiny—the one crafted for them for such a time as this!

The process of becoming a Courageous Girl requires knowing who we are in a community that practices moving through conflict rather than around it, calling us to deeper waters where we find intimacy with God and others. It requires surrender, trust, and obedience. All of our journeys are never exactly how we envisioned, but we can surely rest easy knowing that our God is in the business of restoring, renewing, and rebuilding the long devastation of past generations. Be on the alert and stand firm in the faith; be courageous and be strong. Let all that you do be done in love, by His power. The time is now. Are you with me?

I pray that out of his glorious riches he may strengthen you with power through his Spirit in your inner being, so that Christ may dwell in your hearts through faith. And I pray that you, being rooted and established in love, may have power, together with all the Lord's holy people, to grasp how wide and long and high and deep is the love of Christ, and to know this love that surpasses knowledge—that you may be filled to the measure of all the fullness of God. Now to him who is able to do immeasurably more than all we ask or imagine, according to his power that is at work within us, to him be glory in the church and in Christ Jesus throughout all generations, for ever and ever! Amen. (Ephesians 3:16-21, NIV)

Takeaway

Write a list of five ordinary moments with your daughter this last month. Praise God for those moments and recognize the gift they have been to you. Read and consider the *Hands Free Pledge*. Also, try a technology fast with your daughter (you determine the amount of time). Journal about your experiences. What was difficult for you? What did you learn about yourself, about others and about God? Did God reveal anything specific to you? Consider making this fast part of the rhythms in your lives.

Take It a Step Further

Schedule a half-day prayer session. Maybe connect with another mom and go together—not to talk, but to have accountability for the time. Journal, listen, read, walk, and breathe deeply. Engaging in art, like making a collage, can often help the mind and body settle first. If you are up for a stronger challenge, schedule four of these retreats each year. This will be a way not only to model to your daughter how you take time with God, but it will help you pause, reflect, and stay on track with where He is leading you apart from all the other expectations coming your way.

The Hands Free Pledge
Rachel Macy Stafford

I'm becoming Hands Free.
I want to make memories, not to-do lists.
I want to feel the squeeze of my child's arms,
not the pressure of overcommitment.
I want to get lost in conversations with the people I love,
not consumed by a sea of unimportant emails.
I want to be overwhelmed by sunsets that give me hope,
not by overloaded agendas that steal my joy.
I want the noise of my life to be a mixture of laughter
and gratitude,
not the intrusive buzz of cell phones and text messages.
I'm letting go of distraction, disconnection,
and perfection to live a life that is simply,
so very simple, consists of what really matters.
I'm becoming Hands Free.[9]

Conclusion

STARTING A COURAGEOUS GIRLS GROUP

GETTING STARTED

The hardest part of starting anything is...starting. So congratulations! You have stepped over the line, and something is drawing you to begin a Courageous Girls group for your daughter. You are worth it. She is worth it. We have provided you with everything you will need along the way at www.mycourageousgirls.com, and it's *free*. The only thing that is missing is your unique fingerprint, along with the other mamas and daughters in your sphere of influence.

With prayerful consideration, begin by asking who God has already put in your sphere of influence and who in your community wants to grow in their own walk with God as they walk the road of motherhood. Take time to read through the website and explore the lessons. Every lesson intertwines the truths in this book and aligns with the developmental level of your daughter. You will grow as she grows closer to God, you, and other moms and daughters in your group. Just by reading this page, God is already working in you! As you sink into trusting God each step of the way, believing He is with you, going before you, and empowering you to be a catalyst for transforming relationship, the Courageous Girls team is right beside you as your coach! You've got this. On the website, there are questions and answers for you to consider. Feel free to browse that section to become familiar with some of the roadblocks some moms experience. And then send out an invitation for an initial gathering and see which moms say yes!

GO IN TWOS

Jesus was strategic in sending out disciples two by two in the early days of the church. There is biblical wisdom and courage in partnering with another mom to lead alongside you. Not only will you be able to share the initial responsibilities that slowly shift as the group forms and develops, but you will also be modeling community and "co-creating" from the start. Ephesians 4:9-12 says, "Two are better than one because they have a good return for their labor. If either of them falls down, one can help the other one up." I love the practicality of God's Word. Leadership can be hard in and of itself, and leading women has many of its own unique challenges. Consider someone to partner with you and go in two. Who comes to mind as you pray?

Maybe the mom with whom you partner is someone you do not know well but is someone with a different wiring or skill set that will complement the needs and sustainability of your group over time. Or, perhaps this mom is a close friend whom you trust and know will go the long hall with you based on your history together. Either way, make sure you ask God who *He* thinks is the one who should lead with you and listen to His still voice. Then, take intentional risk.

Whether you choose to go two by two or step out on your own, someone will have to make decisions for the group along the way. Every group of sheep needs a shepherd to keep the sheep from wandering aimlessly. Leadership is necessary for every community, so trying to avoid this role is not a good idea. Leadership with integrity is even more essential, and you will find that God will use your obedient yes to grow you, your own faith journey, and your relationship with your daughter as she watches you step out to start this group with her in mind!

NOW WHAT?

Once you have prayed about a co-leader, begin praying about who in your community loves Jesus or has a desire to grow in their spiritual journey alongside their daughter. Read through the variety of links to get you acquainted with the mission of Courageous Girls and sample a few lessons. Women at all stages of their journey are welcome to join and watch how God moves.

Once you have commitments from mamas, it is ideal to have the moms read this book prior to launching your group, perhaps as a group, as a way to go deeper in relationship. Having an additional book study together with prayer and dialogue will only help you go deeper together.

It's time to stand up for your daughter and lead her well. There is no better way to do this than with other moms and daughters over the course of a long, committed journey. This is where being wrapped *in courage* really counts. God is with you.

Scriptures

2 Corinthians 5:17—Therefore, if anyone is in Christ, he is a new creation. The old has passed away; behold, the new has come.

1 Peter 2:9—But you are a chosen race, a royal priesthood, a holy nation, a people for his own possession, that you may proclaim the excellencies of him who called you out of darkness into his marvelous light.

Galatians 2:20—I have been crucified with Christ. It is no longer I who live, but Christ who lives in me. And the life I now live in the flesh I live by faith in the Son of God, who loved me and gave himself for me.

John 15:15—No longer do I call you servants, for the servant does not know what his master is doing; but I have called you friends, for all that I have heard from my Father I have made known to you.

John 1:12—But to all who did receive him, who believed in his name, he gave the right to become children of God.

Romans 8:17—And if children, then heirs—heirs of God and fellow heirs with Christ, provided we suffer with him in order that we may also be glorified with him.

Colossians 3:3—For you have died, and your life is hidden with Christ in God.

Galatians 3:26—For in Christ Jesus you are all sons of God, through faith.

Romans 8:1—There is therefore now no condemnation for those who are in Christ Jesus.

Philippians 3:20—But our citizenship is in heaven, and from it we await a Savior, the Lord Jesus Christ

1 Corinthians 12:27—Now you are the body of Christ and individually members of it.

1 Corinthians 6:19-20—Or do you not know that your body is a temple of the Holy Spirit within you, whom you have from God? You are not your own, for you were bought with a price. So glorify God in your body.

Ephesians 2:10—For we are God's masterpiece, created to do good works which God prepared in advance for us to do.

Ephesians 4:24—And to put on the new self, created after the likeness of God in true righteousness and holiness.

John 3:16—For God so loved the world, that he gave his only Son, that whoever believes in him should not perish but have eternal life.

Endnotes

INTRODUCTION

1. Thralls, B., Lynch, J., and McNicol, B. (2011, 2016). *The Cure. What if God isn't who you think He is and neither are you?* Pheonix, AZ: Trueface.

2. Orenstein, P. (2016). *Girls & Sex: Navigating the complicated landscape.* New York, NY: Harper Collins Publishing.

3. *Weissbourd, R. Ross, T. Anderson, Cashin, A., and McIntyre, J. (2017). "The Talk: How Adults Can Promote Young People's Healthy Relationships and Prevent Misogyny and Sexual Harassment"* Harvard University: Making Caring Common Project. https://mcc.gse.harvard.edu/thetalk.

4. Wallace, K. (February 13, 2015). *Kids as young as 5 concerned about body image,* **CNN.** www.cnn.com/2015/02/13/living/feat-body-image-kids-younger-ages/index.htm.

5. Thralls, B., Lynch, J., and McNicol, B. (2016). *The Cure & Parents.* San Clemente, CA: CrossSection.

CHAPTER 1

1. Browne, B. (2007). *I Thought It Was Just Me: Women Reclaiming Power and Courage in a Culture of Shame,* New York, NY: Penguin Publishing House.

2. Bultnamn, Theology of the New Testament, 1:220-22; R. Jewett, Paul's Anthropological Terms; T. Song, NIDNITT, 2:80-84; H. W. Wolff, Anthropology of the Old Testament, pp. 40-58

3. Lucado, M. (1997). *You are Special.* Wheaton, IL: Crossway Publishing.

4. Leaf, C., (2013). *Switch on Your Brain.* Grand Rapids, MI: Baker Books.

5. Landreth, G., Bratton, S. Kellam, T. & Blackars, S. (2006). *Child Parent Relationship Therapy: A 10 Session Filial Therapy Model for Training Parents.* Taylor & Francis Group, LLC. (New York: Rutledge).

CHAPTER 2

1. Harville, H. (1988, 2008). *Getting the Love You Want: a guide for couples.* New York, NY: Henry Hold and Company, LLC.

2. Ortberg, J. (April 15, 2017). *In Between Despair and Joy.* http://www.faithgateway.com/in-between-despair-and-joy/#.Ww4YDJPwZE4.

3. Battistelli, F. (2017). *If We're Honest.* https://genius.com/Francesca-battistelli-if-were-honest-lyrics.

4. Landreth, G., Bratton, S. Kellam, T. & Blackars, S. (2006). *Child Parent Relationship Therapy: A 10 Session Filial Therapy Model for Training Parents.* Taylor & Francis Group, LLC. (New York: Rutledge).

CHAPTER 3

1. Brown, B. (2010). *The power of vulnerability.* www.ted.com/talks/brene_brown_on_vulnerability.

2. Sax, L. (2005, 2017). *Why Gender Matters: What parents and teachers need to know about the emerging science of sex differences.* New York, NY: Penguin Random House.

3. Beattie, M. (1992). *Codependent No More.* Center City, MN: Hazleton.

4. Siegel, D., Payne Bryson, T. (2011). *The Whole Brain Child: 12 Revolutionary Ways to Nurture Your Child's Developing Brain.* New York, NY: Penguin Random House, Inc.

5. Siegel, D. (2017). "Flipping Your Lid" (Online Video), www.heartmindonline.org/resources/daniel-siegel-flipping-your-lid.

6. Van der Kolk, B. (2014). *The Body Keeps Score: Brain, mind, and body.* New York, NY: Penguin Random House, Inc.

7. Niequist, S. (2016) *Present Over Perfect: Leaving behind frantic for simpler, more soulful way of living.* Grand Rapids, MI: Zondervan, p. 85.

8. Jantz, G. (1995, 2002). *Hope, Help, and Healing for Eating Disorders: A Whole Person Approach for Treatment of Anorexia, Bulimia, and Disordered Eating.* Colorado Springs, CO: Waterbrook Press.

ENDNOTES

CHAPTER 4

1. Mccarthy, L. (2018). *What Babies Learn in the Womb*. Parenting.com. www.parenting.com/article/what-babies-learn-in-the-womb.

2. Batterson, M. (2015). *If: Trading Your If Only Regrets for God's What If Possibilities*. Grand Rapids, MI: Baker Publishing Group.

3. Thralls, B., Lynch, J., and McNicol, B. (2011, 2016). *The Cure. What if God isn't who you think He is and neither are you?* Pheonix, AZ: Trueface.

4. Dearborn, K. (1999). Class Lecture in *Women in Christianity*. Seattle Pacific University, Seattle, WA.

5. Turner, A. (April 2, 2017). *Meditation 101: The Neuroscience of Why Meditation Works*. Huffington Post. www.huffingtonpost.com/ashley-turner/how-meditation-works_b_4702629.html.

6. Sieber, W. (2017). Lecture from *Calming an Overactive Brain* Workshop. Portland, OR. Institute for Brain Potential.

7. Loyd-Jones, S. (2006). *The Jesus Storybook Bible: Every story whispers His name*. Grand Rapids, MI: ZonderKIDZ.

8. *Bible dictionary*. www.biblestudytools.com/dictionaries/.

9. Thralls, B., Lynch, J., and McNicol, B. (2016). *The Cure & Parents*. San Clemente, CA: CrossSection. pp. 16, 18.

10. Brown, B. (2012). *Daring Greatly: How the Courage to be Vulnerable Transforms the Way We Live, Love, and Parent*. New York, NY: Penguin Publishing House.

CHAPTER 5

1. (2018). Online. dictionary.com.

2. Parrotts, L. & Parrotts, L. (2015). *Saving Your Marriage Before It Starts*. Grand Rapid, MI: Zondervan.

3. Hillsong. (2013). *Oceans*. Zion Album. https://genius.com/Hillsong-united-oceans-where-feet-may-fail-lyrics.

4. Thralls, B., Lynch, J., and McNicol, B. (2016). *The Cure & Parents*. San Clemente, CA: CrossSection.

5. Eric M. (2016). *Seven Women: And the secret of their greatness*. Nashville, TN: Thomas Nelson.

6. Hart, A, and Hart Frejd, S. (2011). *The Digital Invasion: How technology is shaping you and your relationships*. Grand Rapids, MI: Baker Books.

7. Van Dyke, S. (May 3, 2016). *Humans only able to maintain five relationships in their inner-circle, 150 in their outer-circle: study*. National Post. http://nationalpost.com/news/world/humans-only-able-to-maintain-five-relationships-in-their-inner-circle-and-150-in-their-outer-circle-study-finds.

8. Moore, B. (2013). *So Long Insecurity: You've been a bad friend to us*. Tyndall House Publishers.

9. DeMoss Wolgemuth, N., & Gresh, D. (2008, 2018) *Lies Young Women Believe and the Truth that Sets Them Free*. Chicago, IL: Moody Publishers.

10. Steinmetz, K. (March 27, 2017). *Beyond He or She: How a new generation is redefining the meaning of gender*. TIME.

11. Mineo, L. (April 11, 2017). *Good Genes Are Nice, But Joy Is Better*. The Harvard Gazette. https://news.harvard.edu/gazette/story/2017/04/over-nearly-80-years-harvard-study-has-been-showing-how-to-live-a-healthy-and-happy-life/.

12. Bonhoeffer, D. (1954). *Life Together: The Classic Exploration of Faith in Community*, HarperCollins Publishers: New York, NY.

13. Brown, B. (2012). *Daring Greatly: How the Courage to be Vulnerable Transforms the Way We Live, Love, and Parent*. New York, NY: Penguin Publishing House.

14. Cloud, H., & Townsend, J. (2017). *Boundaries Updated and Expanded Edition: When to Say Yes, How to Say No to Take Control of Your Life*. Grand Rapids, MI: Zondervan.

15. Landreth, G., Bratton, S. Kellam, T., & Blackars, S. (2006). *Child Parent Relationship Therapy: A 10 Session Filial Therapy Model for Training Parents*. Taylor & Francis Group, LLC. (New York: Rutledge).

CHAPTER 6

1. Taylor, L. (2000). *Core Values Index*. Seattle, WA: Taylor Protocols Inc.

2. Canary & Messman. (2000) *The Language of Topical Conflict in Everyday Relationships: A Micro-Macro Analysis*. http://citation.allacademic.com/

meta/p_mla_apa_research_citation/2/3/3/8/4/pages233840/p233840-26. php.

3. Gottman, J. (2015). *Seven Principles for Making Marriage Work.* New York, NY: Penguin Random House.

4. Keller, T. (March 6, 2016). *Hope Beyond the Walls of the World.* You Tube. https://www.youtube.com/watch?time_continue=2668&v=SD5LYJ3us0U.

5. Thralls, B., McNicol, B., and Lynch, J. (2005). *Behind the Mask: Reversing the Process of Unresolved Life Issues.* Phoenix, AZ: Leadership Catalyst.

6. Landreth, G., Bratton, S., Kellam, T., & Blackars, S. (2006). *Child Parent Relationship Therapy: A 10 Session Filial Therapy Model for Training Parents.* Taylor & Francis Group, LLC. (New York: Rutledge).

7. (2018). Online. dictionary.com.

8. Cloud, H. (2010). *Necessary Endings: The employees, businesses, and relationships that all of us have to give up in order to move forward.* New York, NY: Harper Collins Publisher.

9. Barton, R.H. (2006) *Sacred Rhythms: Arranging Our Lives for Spiritual Transformation.* Downers Grove, IL: Intervarsity Press.

10. Decety, J., & Ickes, W. (Eds.). (2009). *Social neuroscience. The social neuroscience of empathy.* Cambridge, MA, US: MIT Press.

11. *NASA'.* The Bible Study Tools. Online. lexicons/hebrew/kjv/nasa.html.

12. Tracey. S. (2005). *Mending the Soul: Understanding and Healing Abuse.* Grand Rapids, MI: Zondervan.

13. To explore your own CVI, go to www.livingwholehearted.com or read more on the www.mycourageousgirls.com, Year 3 Curriculum.

14. See www.mycouragourageous girls for definitions of abuse.

CHAPTER 7

1. Moore, B. (2008) *Esther: It's Tough Being a Woman.* Nashville, TN: LifeWay Christian Resource.

2. de Becker, G. (1997). *The Gift of Fear and Other Survival Signals that Protect Us from Violence.* New York, NY: Random House Inc.

3. Raivich, K., & Shatte, A., (2002). *The Resilience Factor: 7 Keys to Finding Your Inner Strength and Overcoming Life's Hurdles.* New York, NY: Broadway Books.

4. Wolfe, J and K. (2016). *Hope Heals.* Grand Rapids, MI: Zondervan. pp. 164-165.

5. Burstein, D. (2013). *Fast Future.* Boston, MA: Beacon Press.

6. Wilson, Lonsway, Archambault, Hopper. (Nov. 2016). *Understanding the Neurobiology of Trauma and Implications for Interviewing Victims.* (Online). www.evawintl.org/Library/DocumentLibraryHandler.ashx?id=842.

7. Landreth, G., Bratton, S., Kellam, T., & Blackars, S., 2006. *Child Parent Relationship Therapy: A 10 Session Filial Therapy Model for Training Parents.* Taylor & Francis Group, LLC. (New York: Rutledge).

CHAPTER 8

1. A sexual timeline is a linear account of experiences that formed your views of gender sexuality and the relationship between the two.

2. Tracey. S. (2005). *Mending the Soul: Understanding and Healing Abuse.* Grand Rapids, MI: Zondervan.

3. Orenstein, P. (2016). *Girls & Sex: Navigating the complicated landscape.* New York, NY: Harper Collins Publishing, p. 19.

4. Zimbardo, P., and Duncan, N. (2011). *The Demise of Guys: Why Boys Are Struggling and What We Can Do About It.*

5. Hart, A., and Hart Frejd, S. (2011). *The Digital Invasion.* Grand Rapids, MI: Baker Books.

6. Sax, L. (2005, 2017). *Why Gender Matters: What parents and teachers need to know about the emerging science of sex differences.* New York, NY: Penguin Random House.

7. Haidt, J. (Oct. 26, 2017) *The Fragile Generation.* New York University Stern School of Business.(Online) http://www.stern.nyu.edu/experience-stern/faculty-research/the-fragile-generation-jonathan-haidt.

8. Dillows, L., and Pintus, L. (2009). *Intimate Issues: Twenty-One Questions Christian Women Ask About Sex.* Colorado Springs, CO: Waterbook Press.

9. Orenstein, P. (2016). *Girls & Sex: Navigating the Complicated Landscapte.* New York, NY: Harper Collins Publishing.

10. Weissbourd, R. Ross Anderson, T., Cashin, A., and McIntyre, J. (2017). *The Talk: How Adults Can Promote Young People's Healthy Relationships and*

Prevent Misogyny and Sexual Harassment. Harvard University: Making Caring Common Project. https://mcc.gse.harvard.edu/thetalk.

11. Wallace, K. (February 13, 2015). *Kids as young as 5 concerned about body image,* CNN. www.cnn.com/2015/02/13/living/feat-body-image-kids-younger-ages/index.htm.

12. Regulating one's sexuality is a key component of the sex addiction recovery work I have been doing for years with couples. Men and women, who have never taken time to find healthy ways to meet their legitimate God-given needs for emotional intimacy, experience anger, disconnection, stress, and loneliness. If their legitimate needs are not met, they will try to meet them in illegitimate ways by turning to patterns that are dangerous and destructive for the brain such as masturbation, pornography, and extramarital affairs.

13. (2018). Online. dictionary.com.

14. A sexual timeline is a linear account of experiences that formed your views of gender, sexuality, and the relationship between the two.

CHAPTER 9

1. Ortberg, J. (2015). *All the Places to God: How Will You Know? God has placed before you an open door. What will you do?* Carol Stream, IL: Tyndall House Publishers, Inc. pp. 61-62.

2. Lewis, C. S. *(1942, 1996). The Screwtape Letters.* New York, NY: Harper Collins Publishers.

3. Crouch, A. (2016). *Strong and Weak: Embracing Life of Love, Risk and True Flourishing.* InterVarstiy Press. Downers Grove, IL: InterVarsity Press.

4. Crouch, A. (2009). *Culture Making: Recovering Our Creative Calling.* InterVarstiy Press. Downers Grove, IL: InterVarsity Press.

5. Terkeurst, Lisa. (2014). *My Best Yes: Making Wise Decisions in the Midst of Endless Demands.* Nashville, TN: Nelson Books.

6. David Crowder Band. *How He Loves.* Church Music Album. https://genius.com/David-crowder-*band-how-he-loves*-lyrics.

7. Brown, B. (2010). *The Gifts of Imperfection: Let Go of Who You Think You're Supposed to Be and Embrace Who You Are.* Center City, Minnesota: Hazelden.

8. Gladwell, M. (2013). *Dave & Goliath: Underdogs, Misfits, and the Art of Battling Giants.* New York, NY: Little, Brown and Company.

9. Brown, B. (2010). *The Gifts of Imperfection: Let Go of Who You Think You're Supposed to Be and Embrace Who You Are.* Center City, Minnesota: Hazelden.

CHAPTER 10

1. Barton, R. (2006). *Sacred Rhythms: Arranging Our Lives for Spiritual Transformation.* Downers Grove, IL: InterVarsity Press.

2. Niequist, S. (2016) *Present Over Perfect: Leaving behind frantic for simpler, more soulful way of living.* Grand Rapids, MI: Zondervan, p. 85.

3. Siegel, D. (2017). "Flipping Your Lid" (Online Video), www.heartmindonline.org/resources/daniel-siegel-flipping-your-lid.

4. Lehman, K. (2011). *It's Your Kid, Not a Gerbil: Creating a Happier & Less-Stressed Home.* Carole Stream, IL: Tyndall House Publishers.

5. Swenson, R. (2004) *Margin: Restoring Emotional, Physical, Financial, and Time Reserves to Overloaded Lives.* Colorado Springs, CO: NavPress.

6. Brown, S. *The Science of Play.* National Institute for Play. Carmel Valley, Calif. (Online). http://www.nifplay.org/.

7. Landreth, G., Bratton, S., Kellam, T., & Blackars, S., 2006. *Child Parent Relationship Therapy: A 10 Session Filial Therapy Model for Training Parents.* Taylor & Francis Group, LLC. (New York: Rutledge).

8. Mother Teresa. (1996). Mother Teresa: In My Own Words. *Linguori, MO: Linguori Publications.*

9. Stafford, R. (2013). *Hands Free Mama.* Grand Rapids, MI: Zondervan.